Medieval Islamic
Sectarianism

PAST IMPERFECT

Past Imperfect presents concise critical overviews of the latest research by the world's leading scholars. Subjects cross the full range of fields in the period ca. 400—1500 CE which, in a European context, is known as the Middle Ages. Anyone interested in this period will be enthralled and enlightened by these overviews, written in provocative but accessible language. These affordable paperbacks prove that the era still retains a powerful resonance and impact throughout the world today.

Director and Editor-in-Chief
Simon Forde, *'s-Hertogenbosch*

Production
Ruth Kennedy, *Adelaide*

Cover Design
Martine Maguire-Weltecke, *Dublin*

Medieval Islamic Sectarianism

Christine D. Baker

British Library Cataloguing in Publication Data
A catalogue record for this book is available from the British Library

© **2019, Arc Humanities Press, Leeds**

ISBN (print): 9781641890823
e-ISBN (PDF): 9781641890830
e-ISBN (EPUB): 9781641890847

www.arc-humanities.org
Printed and bound by CPI Group (UK) Ltd, Croydon, CR0 4YY

Contents

Acknowledgements and a Note on Transliteration. vii

Timeline ix

Introduction 1

Chapter 1. When did Sunnism Become Orthodox?. 17

Chapter 2. Non-Sunni Islams Before the
Tenth Century 27

Chapter 3. The Fatimids and Isma'ili Shi'ism
in North Africa. 37

Chapter 4. The Buyids and Shi'ism in Baghdad 59

Conclusion: Reactions to the Shi'i Century. 77

Glossary of Key Terms 91

Further Reading 103

Acknowledgements and a Note on Transliteration

While all errors are my own, there are many people who aided me while I worked on this project. I would especially like to thank Denise Spellberg, my PhD advisor, for her support and intellectual assistance. Kamran Aghaie, A. Azfar Moin, Stephennie Mulder, Alison Frazier, and Eric Hanne also provided invaluable comments on the work during various stages of its production. I am also grateful to Daisie Huang, who read the manuscript innumerable times and helped me make sense of my ideas when I feared that they made sense to no one. My gratitude also goes to Kate Wood, who provided a space to think and write when I needed one. Thanks to Kim Giles and Vanessa Heggie, friends and advocates, each in their own way. I would not have been able to write this without Indiana University of Pennsylvania (IUP), which has given me a supportive academic home; I especially want to thank Erin Conlin, Rachel Sternfeld, Nicole Goulet, and Lori Labotka at IUP for their encouragement as I worked on the final manuscript. Finally, I need to thank my parents: Lorraine and Frank LaFrazia, who are my constant champions.

In the interest of simplicity, I have not indicated all of the diacritical markings from transliterating Arabic into Latin script. Instead, following *The Chicago Manual of Style*, I have only marked the Arabic letter *hamza* (') and *'ayn* (').

Timeline

224–651	Sassanid Empire
ca. 570	Birth of the Prophet Muhammad
632	Death of the Prophet Muhammad
632–634	Reign of Abu Bakr, first of the *Rashidun* caliphs
634–644	Reign of 'Umar al-Khattab, second of the *Rashidun* caliphs
644–656	Reign of 'Uthman, third of the *Rashidun* caliphs
656–661	Reign of 'Ali b. Abi Bakr, third of the *Rashidun* caliphs
657	Battle of Siffin between forces of 'Ali and Mu'awiya, leads to the emergence of the *Kharijis*
661–750	'Umayyad rule in Syria
680	Husayn b. 'Ali, the third Imam, dies at the Battle of Karbala
740	Zayd b. 'Ali, the fifth Imam, dies during an unsuccessful uprising against the 'Umayyads in Kufa, leading to the emergence of the Zaydi Shi'is
749–750	'Abbasid Revolution
750–1258	'Abbasid rule
762	Death of Isma'il ibn Ja'far al-Sadiq, beginning the division between Isma'ili and Twelver Shi'is
800–909	Aghlabid rule in North Africa

833–847	*Mihna* of the 'Abbasid caliph al-Ma'mun
909–1171	Fatimid rule in North Africa (later, also Egypt, Syria, Palestine, Mecca, Medina, and Yemen)
909–934	Reign of first Fatimid caliph, al-Mahdi
929	'Umayyads in Spain declare a caliphate
934	First Buyid amir, 'Imad al-Dawla, conquers Fars, Iran and establishes dynasty
934–949	Reign of first Buyid amir, 'Imad al-Dawla
934–946	Reign of second Fatimid caliph, al-Qa'im
943	Buyids conquer the Jibal (western Iran)
943–947	*Khariji* rebellion against the Fatimids in North Africa
946–953	Reign of third Fatimid caliph, al-Mansur
949	Buyid ruler 'Adud al-Dawla becomes amir in Fars, Iran
953–975	Reign of fourth Fatimid caliph, al-Mu'izz
955–1055	Buyid rule in Baghdad
969	Fatimids conquer Egypt
971	Fatimids found the city of Cairo
975	Buyid ruler 'Adud al-Dawla seizes power from his cousin in Baghdad (but is soon forced to abdicate)
975–996	Reign of fifth Fatimid caliph, al-'Aziz
979–983	Buyid ruler 'Adud al-Dawla serves as amir in Baghdad
1062	End of the Buyids

Introduction

In part, our understanding of contemporary sectarianism in the Middle East is based on a misunderstanding of the origins and development of Muslim sectarian identities. We tend to view Sunni Islam as the original or orthodox Islam while we portray all other Islams, such as Shi'ism, as heterodox deviations from the original. This book aims to dispel this misconception. While Sunni Islam eventually became politically and numerically dominant, Sunni and Shi'i identities took centuries to develop as independent communities with fully articulated theologies and practices. Rather than seeing Sunnis and Shi'is as having split and never come back together, it is more accurate to view the early Muslim community as espousing a diversity of formulations of Islam that eventually, over centuries, narrowed into the sectarian identities that we can recognize today.

Further, due to modern sectarian conflicts, we tend to assume that enmity and violence have been a constant feature of the Sunni–Shi'i relationship. On the contrary, this book will reveal how the idea of Muslim sectarian hostility developed relatively late in Islamic history by analysing two tenth-century Shi'i dynasties, the Fatimids (909–1171) of North Africa and the Buyids (945–1055) of Iraq and Iran, investigating how they articulated their power, and how local Sunnis reacted to them.

Islamic sectarianism has received a great deal of attention recently due to contemporary events in the Middle East: the collapse of Iraq following the U.S. invasion in 2003, the ongoing Syrian civil war, protests led by Shi'i groups in Yemen and the Gulf States, the tension between Sunni Saudi Arabia and Shi'i Iran, and the rise of extremist Sunni organizations like Daesh/ISIS and al-Qaeda that violently target Shi'i Muslims. These current conflicts in the Middle East, with their emphasis on sectarian identities, have led historians and political scientists to coin the term "sectarianization" as the process by which political actors use aspects of sectarian identity to exacerbate existing conflicts for their own benefit.[1]

It can be easy to blame sectarianism for contemporary and historical conflicts in the Middle East, especially when the causes seem hard to explain. Sectarianism is further complicated because we often use the term to suggest an ancient, deep-seated conflict based in the essentials of culture, which implies that the concept overall is irrational, unchanging, and beyond analysis.[2] Contemporary journalists and politicians often describe conflicts in the Middle East as a simplistic binary that has existed as long as there have been Muslims. To take a handful of examples: in 2007, *Time Magazine* published a cover story entitled, "Sunnis vs. Shi'ites: Why they Hate Each Other." Nearly a decade later, similar articles remain popular, such as *Vice News'* "The Only Thing Iraq's Sunnis and Shias Hate More Than Each Other is the Islamic State" (2015) and *The Independent*'s "Sunni and Shia muslims: Islam's 1400-year-old divide explained" (2016). In a 2013 statement, former U.S. President Barack Obama described the problems in Syria as rooted in "ancient sectarian differences" that would not be easily resolved.[3]

Presenting contemporary conflicts in the Middle East as timeless and unchanging leads to simplistic connections between the present and early Islamic history, which makes analysts miss the very real political, social, and economic roots of current conflicts in the region. Further, the idea of ancient sectarian differences or a fourteen-hundred-year war between Sunnis and Shi'is is inaccurate and misleading. Even when contemporary conflicts involve sectarian movements, these conflicts remain complex and cannot be reduced to ancient hatreds. Viewing these conflicts only through the lens of sectarianism creates misunderstandings and misinterpretations.

Goals

This book asks readers to re-examine their view of the Islamic world and the development of sectarianism in the Middle East. While the book will cover events from the early seventh century through the twelfth century, it is not a survey of Islamic history (although I will provide a very quick overview of historical events below). It is also not a book on Islamic theology or jurisprudence. We will only discuss theology and law to the extent it is necessary to understand the development of sectarian identities and communities.

This book is designed for students and non-experts, so there will be times when, from a specialist perspective, I simplify some complex matters. This choice was deliberate. Scholars have written many excellent books on conversion to Islam, early Shi'ism, the formation of Sunni identity, and how medieval Muslim states used religion to articulate their authority and legitimacy (and I will cite many of them). Surveys of medieval Middle Eastern history designed for students and non-experts, while doing excellent and important work, still often present what renowned historian Richard Bulliet called the "view from the centre":

> The view from the centre portrays Islamic history as an outgrowth from a single nucleus, a spreading inkblot labelled "the caliphate" [...which], in seeking to explain the apparent homogeneity of Islamic society in later centuries, itself something of an illusion, projects back into the days of the caliphate a false aura of uniformity, leaving untold the complex and strife-ridden tale of how Islamic society actually developed.[4]

I hope to provide a view of the development of different forms of sectarian identity that shines a light on the complexity and diversity of early Islamic society.

In this book, I will focus on the tenth century, a period in Middle Eastern history that has often been referred to as the "Shi'i Century," when two Shi'i dynasties rose to power: the Fatimids of North Africa and the Buyids of Iraq and Iran. This era often seems like an anomaly: a period when, for a short time, Shi'is grabbed the wheel of Islamic history but were quickly ousted. Following from this assumption, historians often call the period after the Shi'i Century the "Sunni Revival" because that was when Sunni control was restored. I will argue, however, that these terms present a misleading image of a unified medieval Islam that was predominately Sunni. By looking at the development of terms like Sunni and Shi'i, as well as how they were used by Muslim states, we will learn about the lived experience of countless medieval Muslims.

Historians have long debated about the formation of medieval sectarian identity and I am not the first one to argue that, even in the tenth century, the term Sunni tends to be misleading because religious scholars often used it to indicate whatever they viewed, personally, as Muslim orthodoxy.[5] There have also been excellent critiques of the idea of the Shi'i Century and the Sunni Revival. Richard Bulliet argued that what has been called the Sunni revival was actually only the first stage in the creation of institutions to standardize and disseminate the ideas that would later become the markers of Sunnism[6] and, historian Jonathan P. Berkey noted that, "like many grand historical themes, this one is perhaps a bit too neat and simple."[7] Most recently, art historian Stephennie Mulder observed that, even at the height of the so-called Sunni Revival, Sunnis and Shi'is alike sponsored and venerated shrines dedicated to members of the family of the Prophet later held up as uniquely Shi'i.[8] Despite these sound critiques of the Sunni Revival, the story of the tenth century is still predominantly told as a sectarian narrative, divorced from the overall history of the medieval Islamic world, which helps feed into the overall view of sectarian hostility in Islam.

This book will reintegrate the Shi'i Century into the broader narrative of medieval Islamic history and trace the complexities of sectarian identities in order to dispute Sunnism's early dominance over the concept of orthodoxy and challenge the idea of sectarian conflict dating back to the origins of Islam. Sectarian identities do not conform to a simple binary of Shi'is versus Sunnis. In this book, I will make several interconnecting arguments to prove that this was the case for the tenth-century Islamic world, during the period called the Shi'i Century. First, I will show how even the Shi'i Fatimids made nuanced claims to authority that often followed models from the Sunni 'Abbasid dynasty that had come before them. Fatimid claims to legitimacy did not tend to be based in their Shi'i identity but in broader concepts that would appeal to a wider variety of Muslims. Even the later Fatimids in Cairo, who made more recognizably Shi'i claims to authority, always sought to appeal to a broad constituency of the people they ruled. Second, the Shi'i Buyids also did not base their claims to authority in their Shi'i identity, but rather blended concepts from Sunni, Shi'i, Persian, and Arab modes of authority. Finally, contemporary Sunni reactions to the Fatimids and the Buyids were not necessarily critical of their Shi'i identities. Contemporary commentators often did not highlight the Shi'i identity of either dynasty. Rather it was non-contemporary writers, from the eleventh century and later, who began to focus on sectarian critiques of the Fatimids and Buyids. This shift in portrayals of the Fatimids and the Buyids reveals how Muslim attitudes towards Shi'ism and sectarianism changed from the tenth to the eleventh century.

Islamic History: A Short Overview

This book is not a survey, but it does cover the development of Muslim sectarian identities over a wide geographic and chronological range. Thus, for non-specialists, I will begin with a brief overview of the significant milestones in Islamic history from the seventh through twelfth centuries to serve as a framework to contextualize the book's argument.

The Prophet Muhammad (d. 632) established the first Muslim community in the early seventh century. The Prophet lived in Mecca, in modern Saudi Arabia. Muslims believe that the

Prophet received revelations from God via the Angel Gabriel. But not all Meccans believed in his prophethood: powerful Meccan families persecuted the early Muslims. Thus, in 622, in an event known as the *Hijra,* the Prophet Muhammad and the new Muslim community moved to the nearby settlement of Medina. Invited there by the people of Medina, the Prophet served as both political and religious leader of Medina. The Meccan Arabs considered the Muslims a threat and tried to eliminate the new Muslim community. Eventually, however, due to Muslim military victories and the popularity of the Prophet's message, the Meccans ended their war, converted to Islam, and allowed Muslims access to the *Ka'ba* in Mecca, considered the holiest site in Islam.

After the death of the Prophet, Muslims had to choose a new leader for their community. They did not believe that God would send another Prophet, but they needed to choose someone to fulfil the Prophet's political, religious, and military roles. The community did not agree on a successor. The group we now know as Sunnis (and who, for a lot of the book, I'll call proto-Sunnis), supported the candidacy of the Prophet's closest friend and advisor, Abu Bakr (d. 634). The group we now call Shi'is (who I'll call proto-Shi'is for much of the book), supported the candidacy of the Prophet's cousin and son-in-law, 'Ali b. Abi Talib (d. 661). Abu Bakr's supporters won the debate, making him the leader of the Muslim community. He took the title "caliph," which meant successor to the Prophet. Although the caliphate changed significantly over time, for more than five hundred years, only Arabs descended from the tribe of the Prophet claimed the title. The fact that only an Arab could claim the caliphate became increasingly significant as more non-Arabs converted to Islam in the eighth through tenth centuries.

We identify the conflict over the successor to the Prophet Muhammad as the origin of the Sunni–Shi'i split. The proto-Shi'is get their name because they called themselves the *Shi'at 'Ali,* or the "Partisans of 'Ali." They believed that the Prophet Muhammad had designated 'Ali as his successor. Eventually, they came to believe that 'Ali's power had been deliberately usurped by other members of the first Muslim community. I call this group "proto-Shi'i" (and the group who supported Abu Bakr "proto-Sunni") because it took at least a century, if not more, for Sunnis and Shi'is to begin to develop communities. Modern scholars do not agree on the precise moment when we can consider these groups to be officially the Sunnis and the Shi'is. In chapters one and two, I'll talk a bit about this process, arguing that it actually took far longer than we usually acknowledge.

'Ali eventually became caliph, but it took time. The community selected him as the fourth successor to the Prophet, but his immediate predecessor had been assassinated by an angry mob. After the assassination, 'Ali faced a civil war led by a powerful Meccan family, the 'Umayyads, who blamed him for his predecessor's death. 'Ali's caliphate did not represent a victory for proto-Shi'ism. His conflict with the 'Umayyad family lasted the duration of his short reign and, after 'Ali's death, the 'Umayyads took control over the caliphate.

This earliest period of Islamic history, under the first four successors to the Prophet, holds a special place in Islamic historical memory. Sunnis consider this period to be a kind of golden age; they call it the era of the *Rashidun* or "Rightly-guided" caliphs. From a Sunni perspective, the generation who lived with the Prophet knew how to practise Islam best; after all, they had experienced the Prophet's preaching and guidance first hand. Thus, Sunnis often use the example of the first community, of the Prophet and his Companions, as their example of best practices in Islam. Shi'is also revere the earliest generation of Muslims, but they focus on the Prophet's family, his descendants, and the supporters of 'Ali. Most Shi'is believe that the first three caliphs deliberately stole power from 'Ali despite the Prophet's endorsement of 'Ali as his successor. From a historical perspective, the era of the first four caliphs featured a fair amount of strife over how Muslims should best live, practise their faith, and rule an empire. While Muslims had the Qur'an, the text of God's revelation via the Prophet Muhammad, many questions about how to practise remained unanswered.

Not even the earliest Muslims agreed on the best ways to practise their faith. In addition to their attempts to interpret the Qur'an and the traditions of the Prophet without having a living Prophet, the Muslim community also changed tremendously during the period of the first four caliphs. Muslim armies expanded out of Arabia, ruling over an empire with extensive non-Muslim populations. Their empire grew quickly, conquering territory in Egypt, Syria, Iraq, and Iran. Many of the peoples they conquered were Christians and Jews who did not convert to Islam. The Qur'an forbids forced conversion to Islam and Muslims consider Christians and Jews "People of the Book" because they follow the same God as Muslims. So this new Muslim empire also had to determine how to rule over a diverse population of both Muslims and non-Muslims. In addition, as new peoples converted to Islam and brought their own ideas and interpretations to the faith, it led to further disagreements about the best way to practise Islam and rule the Muslim empire.

The caliphate changed over time as well. The 'Umayyads, the Meccan family who had led the civil war against 'Ali, controlled the caliphate from 661 to 750. They moved the capital of the caliphate from Medina to Damascus, in Syria, and established dynastic rule within their family, which many early Muslims considered a defiance of the tradition of the Prophet. Furthermore, while the first four caliphs had been known for their piety, the 'Umayyads were late converts to Islam and not remembered as particularly pious leaders. In addition, while the first four caliphs had not held themselves apart from the Muslim community, the 'Umayyads started to rule more like medieval kings: building palaces and grand mosques, wearing ceremonial robes, and establishing elaborate court rituals.

Many Muslims felt dissatisfied with 'Umayyad rule and this era saw a proliferation of proto-Shi'i political opposition movements. These movements became more powerful when one of 'Ali's sons, Husayn (d. 680), led a rebellion against the 'Umayyads which ended in his death. Husayn's death changed the character of proto-Shi'i movements: many scholars argue that Husayn's martyrdom shifted anti-'Umayyad political opposition movements into religious movements that eventually developed into Shi'ism.

Husayn's death increased opposition to the 'Umayyads and, eventually, contributed to their overthrow. The 'Abbasids, named for a descendant of the Prophet's uncle 'Abbas (d. 653), organized an anti-'Umayyad revolutionary movement with broad support from proto-Shi'is and Persian converts to Islam. Proto-Shi'is supported them because the 'Abbasids kept the identity of their leader a secret, claiming that they wanted "the best of the people of the Prophet Muhammad" (*al-Rida min Al Muhammad*) to become caliph. Proto-Shi'is assumed this slogan indicated a descendant of 'Ali. Persian Muslims supported the revolution because the 'Umayyads sometimes acted as if Islam was a uniquely Arab religion and often treated Persians like second-class Muslims.

After their revolution, the 'Abbasids disappointed proto-Shi'is with their selection of a descendant of the Prophet's uncle as caliph because most proto-Shi'is only supported descendants of 'Ali and Fatima. Thus, most proto-Shi'is abandoned the 'Abbasids. Persian Muslims tended to remain loyal because the 'Abbasids adopted many aspects of Persian culture. Baghdad, which the 'Abbasids established as their capital, lay within the former Sassanid Empire (224–651), the Persian empire that predated the Muslim conquests. In addition, the 'Abbasid administration hired many Persian Muslims, further Persianising 'Abbasid caliphal ceremonies and the culture of Baghdad. The 'Abbasids remained in power until the thirteenth century, although their power began to decline significantly in the late ninth century and they often held power in name only, especially in provinces distant from Baghdad.

Much of this book will focus on the tenth century, which historians sometimes call the Shi'i century. During this era, two Shi'i dynasties took over the Middle East. First, the Fatimids (909–1171), which began as an underground Shi'i movement in Syria, Yemen, Iran, and southern Iraq, declared a rival caliphate in North Africa in 909. Never before had there been more than one caliph. In addition, at nearly the same time, the Buyids (945–1055), a military family from northern Iran who often worked as mercenaries for local Muslim powers, conquered Baghdad. The Buyids were Shi'i, but they maintained the power and position of the 'Abbasid caliph in Baghdad because they were not Arab and, therefore, could not claim the caliphate.

The Fatimids held power for more than two hundred years, eventually ruling over North Africa, Egypt, portions of Syria and Palestine, as well as the Muslim holy cities of Mecca and Medina. They founded the city of Cairo as their imperial capital and were known for the tolerance of their rule, employing Sunnis, Shi'is, Christians, and Jews in their administration. The Fatimids have also been recognized for their sponsorship of art and education. They founded al-Azhar University, which is considered one of the oldest universities in the world and still in operation today.

The Buyids held power for just over a century. They unified portions of Iraq and Iran which had begun to break away from direct 'Abbasid rule. Taking over Baghdad during a period when the city had been ravaged by civil war and famine, they sought to rebuild the city and restore it to its former glory. At their height, the Buyids held territory in Iran, Iraq, parts of Syria, and the Arabian Gulf, as well as portions of Turkey, Afghanistan, and Pakistan. The Buyids are best remembered by historians for reviving symbols of Persian kingship, harkening back to the era before Islamic rule.

The Buyids were conquered in 1055 while the Fatimids maintained their power until 1171. But this century or so—the time from the fall of the Buyids in 1055 to the end of the Fatimids in 1171—was a period of remarkable disunity and political disintegration in Middle Eastern history. Competing political dynasties divided the region, but the eleventh and twelfth centuries also featured an influx and eventual takeover of Turkic armies from Central Asia, in addition to the invasion of European Crusader forces trying to reconquer Jerusalem.

The Buyids lost their territories to two Turkic dynasties from Central Asia: the Ghaznavids (977–1186) and the Seljuks

(1037–1194). Mahmud of Ghazna (d. 1030), the founder of the Ghaznavids, ruled Afghanistan and expanded into Buyid territory in northern Iran. The Buyids lost Baghdad due to in-fighting within the family. The last Buyid leader asked the Seljuks, a Turkic military confederation that had moved into Iraq, for assistance against a rival. The Seljuk commander, Tughrul Beg (d. 1063), came to Baghdad, but instead of helping the Buyids, he took control over the city and founded the Seljuk dynasty in 1055. The Seljuks eventually ruled much of Iraq, Anatolia, and Syria while the Ghaznavids maintained control over most of Iran and Afghanistan until the late twelfth century.

The end of the Fatimids took another century, but their fall was also partially caused by the Seljuks. Seljuk rule was decentralized: various factions fought for control as they expanded westward. The speed of Seljuk victories in Anatolia, however, led the Byzantine Emperor (who ruled from Constantinople) to ask the pope for military assistance. This request led to the series of wars that we remember as the Crusades. While the Crusaders' goal was the conquest of Jerusalem, they also threatened Fatimid rule, ultimately reconquering Jerusalem from the Fatimids in 1099. Further, Salah al-Din al-Ayyubi (d. 1193), better known as Saladin, served a family of vassals of the Seljuks in Syria. The Fatimids, dealing with their own problems and infighting, sought assistance from those Seljuk vassals in 1164. Saladin, while not the leader of the expedition, assisted and took a leadership role after their victory. In 1169, the Fatimid caliph appointed Saladin to be his *vizier*. Scholars debate why the Shi'i Fatimid caliph appointed Saladin, who was not Shi'i: some claim that the Fatimid caliph underestimated Saladin while others argue that the caliph respected Saladin's "generosity and military prowess." The Fatimids may have thought that promoting Saladin would divide their enemies in Syria. Regardless, Saladin became *vizier* and, when the reigning Fatimid caliph died in 1171, Saladin proclaimed his own rule over Fatimid territory.

Neither Saladin nor the Seljuk rulers were Arab, thus none of them claimed the caliphate. Instead, both Saladin and the Seljuks presented themselves as the defenders of the 'Abbasid caliph and made shrewd alliances with urban Sunni religious leaders. These strategies allowed the new Turkic dynasties to claim their legitimacy as protectors of the caliph and of orthodox Sunni Islam. Their takeover and use of Sunni orthodoxy as a legitimization tool also led them to demonize the Shi'i dynasties that had preceded them. This process, in large part, created the idea of Sunni–Shi'i hostility that we think of as timeless today.

Power, Authority, Legitimacy, and a Problem of Sources

This book analyses the crystallization of Sunni and Shi'i identity and how these Muslim sects developed over time. But, in order to do that, we will focus on analysing how medieval dynasties articulated their authority and legitimacy. Deconstructing how medieval rulers claimed power (which is what we mean by "authority and legitimacy") allows us to see what was important to the people over whom these medieval dynasties ruled. This methodology might seem like an indirect way of approaching how medieval Muslim communities defined their sectarian identities. But religious identity played a significant role in medieval political legitimacy—medieval rulers often claimed to be chosen by God in some way—so examining how these rulers used their faith to talk about their right to rule gives us insight into what the people they ruled would have thought about their faith. In addition, many of the peoples of the medieval Islamic world did not leave behind sources attesting to their feelings about sectarianism, so this approach allows us to glimpse their views on the matter and not only focus on the opinions of elite religious scholars.

But what, exactly, do we mean when we talk about power, authority, and legitimacy? Whole books have been devoted to this very topic but, stated simply, authority is a kind of power. Power, most broadly, can be considered the "force by means of which you can oblige others to obey you" while authority "is the *right* to direct and command, to be listened to or obeyed by others. Authority requests power. Power without authority is tyranny."[9] So, a state (especially one with an army) has the *power* to create law, collect taxes, go to war, and enforce obedience. But they seek the *authority* to do so by making arguments that they have the *right* to hold power. There are different kinds of authority, of course. We will focus on the authority of the caliph, but other people held different types of authority in the medieval Islamic world: people like military leaders and religious scholars. The caliph needed these people to support his authority.

Legitimacy is linked with authority: it encompasses the system of government used to claim the right to exercise authority. Governments claim legitimacy in different ways. For example, modern democracies base their legitimacy on elections. The government has the right to tax, make laws, and go to war because it was elected by a majority of the people. In the medieval world, rulers often based their legitimacy on the spiritual authority of God. The king/caliph/emperor had the right to rule because he was chosen and supported by God.

In medieval societies, rulers made clear statements claiming their right to rule and used symbolic ways of communicating their authority through art, architecture, and ceremony. As the Muslim empire expanded, the ways that the caliphs claimed legitimacy changed. At first, when the Muslim community was small and homogenous, it was easier: even if not everyone always agreed, the community knew the first four caliphs for their loyalty to the Prophet and the piety of their faith. These two attributes, plus the fact that they were selected by leaders within the community, gave them legitimacy in the eyes of most Muslims.

Furthermore, when discussing authority and legitimacy, it is significant to consider the *audience* for these claims. Even medieval rulers needed to make claims that would appeal to a wide variety of constituencies. As the Muslim empire expanded to rule over a more heterogeneous population, most of which was *not* Muslim, they had a harder task. Non-Muslims would not grant the caliph legitimacy because of his piety or relationship with Islam. The caliph had to act how people would expect a medieval ruler to act. In general, the 'Umayyads and the 'Abbasids (as well as the Fatimids and Buyids) borrowed ways that pre-Islamic empires, like the Byzantines, the successors of the eastern Roman Empire, and the Persian Sassanid dynasty, had claimed their legitimacy.[10] Since the Byzantines and the Sassanids had ruled over the region for centuries, they had established protocols for claiming authority that would be recognizable by the diverse peoples of the region. Muslim dynasties based a lot of their authority on Islam, but also used architecture, regalia, rituals, and ceremony that would be recognized as markers of legitimacy to a non-Muslim audience.

Despite the ways that the caliph would need to appeal to a wide variety of peoples, both Muslim and non-Muslim, to maintain his power, historians tend to focus on how religious scholars responded to the caliph. We do this because religious scholars tend to be the group we know the most about in medieval Muslim society: they wrote most of the sources that survive. So we know a lot about what they thought about sectarian identities, but we do not always have clear ways to find out what other people might have thought. Most people, especially non-elites, did not leave behind written sources, so it can be difficult to determine their views. In this book, we will examine how the Fatimids and Buyids used or did not use their sectarian identities to claim legitimacy in order to read between the lines to see what kinds of messages were acceptable to broad medieval audiences.

The era of the Fatimids and the Buyids offers a unique opportunity to examine ideas of identity in medieval Islamic society because the tenth century witnessed tectonic shifts within the very idea of Muslim society. First, it was the period when the Middle East became predominately Muslim for the first time, bringing more non-Arabs (and their ideas) into the Muslim faith. Second, Fatimid and Buyid domination of the region represented a massive break with the earlier unity of the Islamic world under one caliph. And third, because the Fatimids and Buyids identified as Shi'i, their competition and the reaction of Sunni political elites and religious scholars helped crystallize different forms of sectarian identity.

Analysing how the Fatimids and Buyids, two Shiʿi dynasties, claimed their legitimacy over a diverse population of Muslims and non-Muslims allows us to glimpse the myriad of ways that the people of the tenth century viewed themselves and their identities. The caliph had to express his right to rule in a way that resonated with the people he ruled. In the Shiʿi century, we might expect medieval Muslim rulers to foreground their sectarian identities, but they did not. We also might expect that critiques of these Shiʿi states would focus on their Shiʿi identity, but they did not. This book looks at what that can tell us about sectarianism and medieval Islamic society.

Notes

[1] Nader Hashemi and Danny Postel, eds., *Sectarianization: Mapping the New Politics of the Middle East* (Oxford: Oxford University Press, 2017), 4–5.

[2] Toby Matthiesen, *Sectarian Gulf: Bahrain, Saudi Arabia, and the Arab Spring that Wasn't* (Stanford: Stanford University Press, 2013).

[3] "Statement by the President on Syria," August 31, 2013, https://obamawhitehouse.archives.gov/the-press-office/2013/08/31/statement-president-syria

[4] Richard Bulliet, *Islam: The View from the Edge* (New York: Columbia University Press, 1995), 7.

[5] Marshall G. S. Hodgson, *Venture of Islam*, vol. 1: *The Classical Age of Islam* (Chicago: University of Chicago Press, 1977), 278.

[6] Bulliet, *View from the Edge*, 127.

[7] Jonathan P. Berkey, *The Formation of Islam: Religion and Society in the Near East, 600–1800* (Cambridge: Cambridge University Press, 2002), 189–193.

[8] Stephennie Mulder, *The Shrines of the ʿAlids in Medieval Syria: Sunnis, Shiʿis, and the Architecture of Coexistence* (Edinburgh: Edinburgh University Press, 2014), 14.

[9] Jacques Maritain, *Man and the State* (Chicago: Chicago University Press, 1951), 126, as quoted in George Makdisi, "Authority in the Islamic Community," *La Notion d'autorité au Moyen Age: Islam, Byzance, Occident* (Paris: Presses universitaires de France, 1982), 117.

[10] Aziz al-Azmeh, *Muslim Kingship: Power and the Sacred in Muslim, Christian, and Pagan Polities* (London: I. B. Tauris, 2001), ix–x.

Chapter 1

When did Sunnism Become Orthodox?

Our understanding of contemporary sectarianism in the Middle East is based on a misunderstanding of the origins and development of Muslim sectarian identities. In part, the misperception that we can reduce modern conflicts between Sunnis and Shiʻis to the seventh century derives from how we tell the story of the Sunni-Shiʻi split. This narrative derives from the fact that modern Sunnis and Shiʻis *do* trace the origins of their communities back to a seventh-century disagreement over who should succeed the Prophet Muhammad, but that's not the end of the story of the development of Muslim sectarian identities.

In this chapter, we will discuss how our understanding of Sunni orthodoxy has changed over time. Scholars differ fairly significantly in how they date the emergence and dominance of Sunni orthodoxy. This difference derives from the types of sources that they use. Scholars who rely predominately on sources composed by religious scholars date the dominance of Sunni orthodoxy to the late eighth or ninth centuries. On the other hand, scholars who focus on the institutions that would have helped spread and police ideas of Sunni orthodoxy argue that this process was not yet complete before the twelfth or thirteenth century. I tend to agree with the more institution-minded approach; while ideas of Sunni orthodoxy may have been established amongst religious scholars, we have little evidence that these ideas were important to a broader swath of society until institutions were in place that helped spread and enforce these ideas.

The word orthodoxy comes from the Greek roots *ortho*, meaning straight, and *doxa*, meaning doctrine. Thus, orthodoxy can be understood as the attempt to define what is the proper (or straight) doctrine for a particular faith. From a scholarly perspective (that is, not necessarily the perspective of believers), however, practitioners and followers of a faith *construct* notions of orthodoxy. While we may believe that religious texts came directly from God or prophets, people must still interpret those texts and apply them in their lives. Believers will always have questions about how to best practise their faith that are not directly answered in religious texts; thus, there is a need for interpretation. In many religions, one official form of a faith often comes to be portrayed as orthodox and all the rest depicted as heterodox (from the Greek *heteros*, meaning other, and *doxa*, meaning doctrine).

Because Sunnis represent the majority of today's Muslims, Sunnis generally consider their form of Islam to be orthodox Islam and think of it as the original form from which all other Islams derived. However, this vision of Sunnism assumes a coherence and unity to early Islamic doctrine and practice that is not evident in early Islamic sources. In contrast, medieval sources portray the early Muslim community as diverse and containing many different types of Muslim groups demanding the right to define Islam in their own ways. This diversity will be discussed in detail in chapter two, but we will first analyse when a distinct idea of Sunni identity emerged.

Islam does not have one overarching religious leader, so the question of who has the authority to decide what constitutes orthodoxy and heterodoxy is not a completely straightforward one. Sunni Islam, much like Shiʻism and other types of Islam, developed over time. Neither Sunnism nor Shiʻism can claim to be the original form of Islam; both derive from the earliest communities of Muslims. This chapter will analyse when Muslims came to see Sunni Islam as the orthodox form of Islam, arguing that we should date this idea to the eleventh or twelfth century at the earliest.

The types of sources that modern scholars use to answer the question of when Sunnism constituted Islamic orthodoxy has a tremendous effect on how they answer this question. In general, using religious sources tends to provide an earlier answer: sometime in the late eighth century. Using sources on the kinds of institutions that existed to define, spread, and police Sunni orthodoxy pushes the date forward until the eleventh or twelfth centuries (and sometimes as late as the fourteenth century!). Thus, there is a great deal of variation in the answers to the question of when Sunni orthodoxy became dominant. Significantly, however, scholars do not argue that Sunni orthodoxy was established in the seventh century during the lifetime of the Prophet Muhammad. It took a long time for these ideas to develop and coalesce into distinct communities.

Religious Scholars as the Creators of Sunni Orthodoxy?

The late eighth century, approximately a century after the death of the Prophet, is usually the earliest that modern scholars will argue that we can identify the idea of Sunni orthodoxy. They base this date on the development of a group of religious scholars known as the *ahl al-Sunna* (literally: the people of tradition).[11] The *ahl al-Sunna* were medieval religious scholars who analysed a body of sources called *hadith*, stories about the life of the Prophet Muhammad and his closest Companions, in order to identify clear rules about how Muslims should best practise their faith. The collected body of *hadith*, known as the *Sunna* (Tradition), is where we get the term Sunni. *Hadith* interested the *ahl al-Sunna* because they believed that following the example of the Prophet Muhammad and his earliest Companions provided the best possible blueprint for proper Muslim behaviour.

But this process was not a simple nor straightforward one. Scholars did not necessarily agree on which *hadith* could be trusted. Individual *hadith* had been passed down orally for more than a century before scholars began writing them down. Then, in the ninth century, scholars collected these *hadith* into canonical collections that Muslims referenced when deciding questions of religious law. But during the century or so when scholars collected and transmitted these *hadith* by word of mouth, many suspicious *hadith* had been collected. The *ahl al-Sunna* devoted their scholarly attention to vetting the people who had transmitted *hadith*, arguing that Muslims could only trust *hadith* transmitted by upright Muslims which was based on the scholarly definition of upright. Because the *ahl al-Sunna* collected and vetted *hadith* from about the late eighth century and published what are now considered the canonical Sunni collections of *hadith* in the ninth century, some modern scholars argue that we can date the emergence of the idea of a Sunni community and Sunni orthodoxy to as early as the late eighth/early ninth century.

But there are problems with dating Sunni orthodoxy to the late eighth century. There is a difference between using the term *ahl al-Sunna* and self-awareness and recognition of a broader Sunni identity.[12] How much can we extrapolate a definition of orthodoxy based on religious experts who devoted their lives to studying the Prophet and his Companions to regular Muslims? Do the *ahl al-Sunna* represent a majority of Muslims? Although they constituted a distinct group by the eighth and ninth centuries that had significant influence on the definitions of Sunni orthodoxy, it seems misleading to define the dominance of Sunni orthodoxy based on the date when this small group of experts emerged, especially when no mechanism yet existed for spreading and policing ideas of Sunni orthodoxy. In other words, urban religious scholars may have agreed on a definition of Sunni orthodoxy, but how did they tell regular Muslims about it?

Furthermore, to what degree were Sunni-leaning religious scholars unified before the eleventh century? Historian Daphna Ephrat argued that it was not until the eleventh century that Sunni religious scholars in Baghdad began to consolidate as a "defined and exclusive group." This consolidation derived, in part, from the creation of institutions where these religious scholars could be employed.[13]

Institutions as the Creators of Sunni Orthodoxy?

Instead of using religious sources, some historians take an institutional approach to defining the emergence of Sunni orthodoxy, centring the question of how institutions, such as mosques, schools, and universities, could articulate, spread, and police concepts of Sunni orthodoxy.[14] The argument here is that, without some kind of mechanism for spreading ideas of orthodoxy, it did not matter what a small group of religious scholars considered to be Sunnism. An institutional approach tends to date the creation of Sunni orthodoxy to sometime in the eleventh through fourteenth centuries. As you can see, the institutional approach leads to a much later date for the emergence of a distinct concept of Sunni orthodoxy.

The most significant institution known for spreading concepts of Islamic orthodoxy was the *madrasa*, or Muslim religious college. Before the creation of the *madrasa*, there was no system for systematising and spreading concepts of Sunni orthodoxy. Historians trace the advent of the *madrasa* to patronage by the caliph and other political elites in the eleventh century,[15] after the fall of the Buyids, as a way of training Sunni Muslim bureaucrats to work for the state. Nizam al-Mulk (1018–1092), who served as *vizier* (similar to a chief of staff) for the early Seljuks (who had overthrown the Buyids), helped found a system of state-sponsored *madrasa*s that became known as the *Nizamiyya* and taught the basics of Sunni Islam. Seljuk patronage of the *madrasa* does not appear to have been fuelled by anti-Shi'ism but was due to a desire to support religious scholars who might help legitimise the dynasty.[16]

But, before the *madrasa*, how did people learn about Islam? There was no one institution that had a monopoly on this task before at least the eleventh century. Neither the 'Umayyads nor the 'Abbasids made systemic efforts to spread Islam outside of the military and urban areas.[17] Islamic education tended to be informal and not centrally directed. In cities, mosques served as centres of learning.[18] While, as mentioned above, a distinct class of religious scholars began to emerge in the eighth century, urban Muslims often learned about Islam from popular preachers and storytellers.[19]

The Caliphate as an Arbiter of Sunni Orthodoxy?

While Islam has no one religious leader, in the medieval era, the caliphate came the closest to this position. Caliph literally means successor; the caliph succeeded the Prophet Muhammad as a political leader, commander of the military, and prayer leader for the community. Thus, it might seem logical that the caliph himself would define Sunni orthodoxy.

But the caliphate was an institution like any other: it developed and changed over time. The first caliphs drew from the earliest converts to Islam from the Prophet's tribe, selected by a committee of significant members of the Muslim community. But, starting with the 'Umayyads in the seventh century, the caliphate became a hereditary position. Even so, the 'Umayyads considered themselves to be the creators of religious law and were accepted as such.[20]

The caliphate changed drastically during the early 'Abbasid period. As the 'Abbasid caliph adopted aspects of kingship derived from pre-Islamic Sassanid traditions, the caliphate took on more mythic elements. An institution that had begun in the seventh century as a human successor to the Prophet began to be considered the "shadow of God on earth" by the ninth century. While the first caliphs lived among the Muslim community and did not separate themselves from it, the 'Abbasid caliphs remained aloof and isolated from the people over whom they ruled. The 'Abbasids acted much more like pre-Islamic kings: these ninth-century caliphs had little in common with the first successors to the Prophet Muhammad.

Furthermore, while the caliph's power grew over time, his ability to act as the arbiter of orthodoxy in Islam varied tremendously. It was not a role that he held unchallenged. From the outset of the caliphate, Muslims challenged both the person chosen to lead the community and the degree to which he had power to define Islamic faith and practice.

While, under the 'Umayyads, the caliphs were considered the progenitors of the law, religious scholars—especially the *ahl al-Sunna*—began to challenge this role in the eighth century because they felt they had greater expertise and religious knowledge. By the end of the eighth century, religious scholars argued that *hadith* should be the source of religious law because it empowered them over the caliph.

Individual caliphs tried to break the power of these religious scholars, whom they viewed as trying to usurp the authority of the caliphs by claiming authority over religious matters. For example, in the early ninth century, the 'Abbasid caliph al-Ma'mun (r. 813–833) established a policy called the *Mihna* (usually translated as "trial" or, more extravagantly, "Inquisition") that lasted from about 833 to 847. In the *Mihna*, al-Ma'mun and his successors required all religious scholars employed by the state to adopt certain philosophical and theological positions. This policy, however, caused significant opposition and, in the end, the *Mihna* was seen as a breaking point when the caliph lost the ability to set religious policies.[21]

These power struggles between the 'Abbasid caliphs and urban religious scholars happened throughout the ninth century and were not, in any way, settled by that time. If medieval Muslims could not agree on who had the authority to create Sunni orthodoxy in the ninth century, can we really argue that Sunni orthodoxy was dominant? Further, we still have the problem of the mechanism by which these urban, elite debates over concepts of Sunni orthodoxy would be transmitted to regular Muslims.

Competition within Sunni Islam

Today, there is a fairly high degree of unity within Sunni Islam. While we identify four schools of Sunni Islamic law (or jurisprudence), Hanafism, Shafi'ism, Hanbalism, and Malikism, each of these schools accepts the validity of the others. In other words, you can follow a Maliki interpretation of Sunni Islam and the Hanafis, Shafi'is, and Hanbalis will still consider you to be an orthodox Sunni Muslim. But this position took *centuries* to be accepted. Islamic Studies Professor Jonathan Brown argues that the unification of Sunni identity mostly happened in the eleventh century and afterwards. Before this point, Sunni religious scholars competed fiercely over definitions of orthodoxy, often attacking other forms of Sunni tradition.

In the tenth century, the different schools of Sunni jurisprudence were still in this period of fierce competition. It was not until the mid-eleventh century when different collections of *hadith* (stories about the life of the Prophet and his Companions) became canonized that Sunni religious scholars developed common ground. These collections of *hadith* provided a common reference point for scholars trying to define Sunni practice. This process occurred as the Buyids lost power in Iraq and the Seljuks began to use Sunni identity to claim their right to lead.

Notes

[11] Scott C. Lucas, *Constructive Critics, Hadith Literature, and the Articulation of Sunni Islam: The Legacy of the Generation of Ibn Sa'd, Ibn Ma'in, and Ibn Hanbal* (Leiden: Brill, 2004) and Christopher Melchert, in *The Formation of the Sunni Schools of Law, 9th–10th Centuries C.E.* (Leiden: Brill, 1997).

[12] Christopher Melchert, "The Piety of the Hadith Folk," *The International Journal of Middle Eastern Studies*, 34, no. 3 (August 2002), 425–39.

[13] Daphna Ephrat, *A Learned Society in a Period of Transition: The Sunni 'Ulama' of Eleventh-Century Baghdad* (Albany: State University of New York Press, 2000), 6.

[14] Jonathan Brown, *The Canonization of Al-Bukhari and Muslim: The Formation and Function of the Sunni Hadith Canon* (Leiden: Brill, 2007) and Berkey, *Formation of Islam*.

[15] George Makdisi, *The Rise of Colleges* (Edinburgh: Edinburgh University Press, 1981).

[16] Ephrat, *A Learned Society*, 2–3.

[17] Nehemia Levtzion, "Comparative Study," in *Conversion to Islam* (New York: Holmes & Meier, 1979), 8 and 17.

[18] Makdisi, *The Rise of Colleges*.

[19] Khalil 'Athamina, "Al-Qasas: Its Emergence, Religious Ori-

gin, and Its Socio-Political Impact on Early Muslim Society," *Studia Islamica* 76 (1992), 53–74 at 54. Jonathan Berkey also has a detailed discussion of the origins of *qussas* and their role in early Islamic society in *Popular Preaching and Religious Authority in the Medieval Islamic Near East* (Seattle: University of Washington Press, 2011), 22–32.

[20] Patricia Crone and Martin Hinds, *God's Caliph: Religious Authority in the First Centuries of Islam* (New York: Cambridge University Press, 1986).

21 Melchert argues that, in the ninth century, only Muhtadi and Mu'tamid (through Muwaffaq) had any kind of specific religious policy after the Mihna. See Melchert, "Religious Policies of the Caliphs from al-Mutawakkil to al-Muqtadir, AH 232–295/AD 847–908," Islamic Law and Society 3, no. 3 (1996), 316–42.

Chapter 2

Non-Sunni Islams Before the Tenth Century

It took centuries for a coherent and unified concept of Sunni Islam to develop and even longer for the creation and promulgation of mechanisms to spread and enforce those ideas. During this time, other interpretations of Islam—other Islams—remained popular. Many of these religious movements were linked with political opposition to either the 'Umayyad or 'Abbasid dynasty, both of which were seen by some Muslims as having usurped power from more legitimate leaders.

While, to some extent, we could consider Sunni Islam to be politically dominant before the tenth century and the rise of the Fatimids and the Buyids, these two dynasties did not arise in a vacuum. They developed out of a myriad of political and religious opposition movements popular across the Muslim world. Sunni Islam was also far from unified: it only appears so in retrospect.

This chapter surveys the many forms of Islam popular before the tenth century, focusing on movements that seemed to view themselves as existing outside any kind of developing Sunni consensus. Furthermore, this chapter will argue that, although proto-Shi'ism/Shi'ism was a significant part of political and religious opposition to the 'Umayyads and 'Abbasids, reducing the Islams of this era to a simple binary between Sunni and Shi'i Islam is too simplistic. Sunni and Shi'i Islam developed in tandem, incorporating ideas from other types of non-Sunni and non-Shi'i movements. In addition to proto-Shi'ism and its development into different forms of Shi'ism, this chapter will address two other major types of Muslim religious movements before the tenth century: Kharijism and Khurramism.

The Twelve Imams and Proto-Shi'ism

I have been referring to Shi'ism and Sunnism from before the ninth century as "proto-Shi'ism" and "proto-Sunnism," respectively, because it took quite some time for these beliefs to be defined and communities of believers to coalesce. When we learn about both Sunnism and Shi'ism, we tend to view it from the modern perspective, from which the process by which these communities formed seems much more straightforward than it was at the time.

For example, we tend to define different forms of Shi'ism based on who they consider to be the true Imam. The Imamate is one of the most significant beliefs separating Sunnis and Shi'is. While disagreements exist over the precise definition of the term, Shi'is consider the Imam to be a descendant of the Prophet Muhammad who possesses special religious knowledge (*'ilm*) which allows him to best guide the Muslim community in the absence of the Prophet. Over time, most Shi'is also came to believe that the Imam must be designated (*nass*) by the previous Imam; this designation allowed for the continuation of the community with fewer disagreements over the Imam's identity and also allowed for the transmission of the previous Imam's knowledge to his successor. Today, three main types of Shi'i Islam have survived: Zaydi, Isma'ili, and Twelver.

The history of Shi'ism tends to be defined from the perspective of the present, after most of the debates about the Imamate were settled. We have a fairly tidy narrative of the development of Zaydi, Isma'ili, and Twelver Shi'ism: before there were three distinct forms of Shi'ism, we often called these people who sought to follow the Imam the *Imamiyya*. Broadly, the *Imamiyya* agreed on the identities of the first four Imams: first, 'Ali b. Abi Talib, the cousin and son-in-law of the Prophet Muhammad; second, Hasan, 'Ali's oldest son with Fatima, the daughter of the Prophet; third, Husayn, 'Ali's second son with Fatima; fourth, 'Ali Zayn al-'Abidin, Husayn's son.

After the death of 'Ali Zayn al-'Abidin, one group of *Imami-yya*—who we now call the Zaydis— split off from the rest. The Zaydis followed the Imamate of Zayd, one of the sons of 'Ali Zayn al-'Abidin, which is why we call them Zaydis. The rest of the *Imamiyya* followed one of Zayd's half-brothers.

The story of the split between the groups now known as Isma'ilis and Twelvers was similar: after the death of the sixth Imam, they disagreed on his rightful successor. The Isma'ilis followed his son Isma'il (hence the name) while the Twelvers followed his half-brother. The Twelvers are known as such because they follow a line of twelve descendants of the Prophet Muhammad via 'Ali and Fatima and they believe that the twelfth Imam, Muhammad al-Mahdi, disappeared soon after his birth into a state of spiritual hiding (*ghayba*). Twelvers believe that Muhammad al-Mahdi will return at some future date to begin the end of time. While Twelvers do not believe in any more Imams after Muhammad al-Mahdi, both the Zaydis and the Isma'ilis still follow living descendants of 'Ali and Fatima.

While this looks like a clean, tidy narrative, it ignores a massive number of different proto-Shi'i groups which followed many different candidates to the Imamate before the ninth century. Even students of medieval Islamic history often do not learn much about the complexity of this era because the sources are problematic and the myriad of names and competing groups can be confusing for non-specialists. I want to try to discuss the complexity of this period in a way that is approachable for non-specialists.

The problem with the sources for these proto-Shi'i movements is not trivial. Most of the sources that survive on these early movements come from a genre of writing known as heresiography. Heresiography is the study of heresy, religious ideas that are considered outside the realm of orthodoxy. These heresiographies attempted to collect the names and beliefs of groups that were considered wrong and they are very common in medieval writing. As historian Sean W. Anthony put it, "All Muslim groups that produced theologians also produced heresiography."[22] Heresiographical texts usually take an ahistorical approach to whatever they view as orthodoxy, ignoring the ways in which religious beliefs and practices develop over time and in specific contexts.

Islamic heresiographical texts are further compromised by a famous saying attributed to the Prophet Muhammad known as the *hadith al-tafriqa*: "The Jews divided into seventy-one sects, the Christians into seventy-two sects, and my community will divide into seventy-three sects." Sometimes the *hadith* ends with the sentence "All of them are in hellfire except one religious group." Thus, many heresiographers tried to identify the seventy-two heresies (presuming that their group is the saved one).[23] Modern scholars have sometimes followed this approach, trying to trace the leaders and beliefs of groups for which we often know little more than a name.

Instead of trying to review every proto-Shiʻi movement mentioned in heresiographical sources, I want to follow the approach of historian William F. Tucker, who researched proto-Shiʻism predating the ʻAbbasid revolution in 750.[24] Tucker focused on the groups that developed some of the core beliefs that were later absorbed into Shiʻism (and, sometimes, Sunnism). While this may not be a comprehensive survey of every possible proto-Shiʻi movement, it will provide an overview of some of the diversity in Muslim identity even in the first century after the life of the Prophet Muhammad.

Tucker, focusing on the city of Kufa in Iraq (a known centre of proto-Shiʻi activity) identified at least seven active proto-Shiʻi organizations in the late seventh and early eighth century: the *Sabaʻiyya*, *Kaisaniyya*, *Bayaniyya*, *Hashimiyya*, *Mughiriyya*, *Mansuriyya*, and the *Janahiyya*. You do not need to remember their names, but it is important to know that the followers of these movements were some of the first to engage in Qurʼanic exegesis to find hidden meanings in the Qurʼan via symbolic or allegorical interpretation. Later Shiʻi movements refer to this deeper meaning of the Qurʼan as the *batin*, which means inner or hidden. (Later, *batini* came to be used as a pejorative for Shi'is.) Today, both Sunnis and Shi'is engage in forms of esoteric interpretation of the Qur'an (although they often disagree on those interpretations).

Scholars also credit these proto-Shi'i movements with developing the concept of the *Mahdi* as a messianic figure. Muslims consider the *Mahdi* to be a redeemer who will return before the Day of Judgement to rid the world of evil and usher in an era of justice. The Qur'an does not contain any explicit references to the *Mahdi*, but both Sunnis and Shi'is acknowledge the role he will play in the endtimes. The *Kaisaniyya* probably first preached that a *Mahdi* would someday return: perhaps influenced by Christian messianism, the *Kaisaniyya* refused to acknowledge 'Ali's death. Instead, they believed that he had ascended to heaven and would someday return to usher in the Day of Judgment.

Some of these proto-Shi'i groups did profess ideas that other early Muslims viewed as heretical. For example, some believed that their leaders were capable of magical feats or reincarnation. Some claimed that the Imams were the physical incarnations of God. Later Shi'i movements that survived the seventh and eighth centuries largely rejected these types of beliefs which became known as *ghuluww* or exaggerations.

The later *Imamiyya* groups came to a consensus that the Imam needed to be a descendant of 'Ali and Fatima. But, during this period of proto-Shi'i activity, that was not yet a settled idea. These groups tended to follow a descendant of 'Ali, but some followed his sons and descendants by another woman. Significantly, the *Hashimiyya*, which was the proto-Shi'i group that organized the 'Abbasid revolution, followed Abu Hashim (d. 776), a descendant of 'Ali via another wife. According to *Hashimiyya*/'Abbasid history, Abu Hashim appointed a descendant of the Prophet's uncle, 'Abbas, as his successor, which is why we later know the dynasty that took over from the *Hashimiyya*-led revolution as the 'Abbasids.

In addition to the many proto-Shi'i movements that did not survive the eighth century, the *Imamiyya* also emerged from these broader 'Alid movements. Although, as we discussed in the narrative of the Zaydis, Isma'ilis, and Twelvers, even their emergence was not so neat: it involved a great deal of division among inter-competing groups. Furthermore, while we are ending our discussion of these proto-Shiʻi ʻAlid movements in the mid-eighth century, the issues were not nearly settled by that time. It was during the tenth century, under Ismaʻili Fatimid and Twelver Buyid rule, that different Shiʻi movements (notably the Ismaʻilis and the Twelvers) began to crystallize as distinct movements with clear and separate theologies and practices.

Khariji Movements

The *Khariji*s represent another significant religious movement in early Islamic history. The term *khariji* translates as "those who leave" and derives from their actions at the Battle of Siffin (657), when the caliph ʻAli b. Abi Talib fought the army of Muʻawiya, the governor of Damascus who later became the first ʼUmayyad caliph. The *Khariji*s began the battle as supporters of ʻAli but abandoned his cause during the battle. The Arabic verb *kharaja*, from which we get *Khariji*, means "to leave"; they are named after their abandonment of ʻAli at Siffin.

The name *Khariji* is controversial. The *Khariji*s used different terms to describe themselves, the most common being *shurat* ("exchanger") or *Muhakkima*. *Shurat*, or exchanger, came from their belief that they would exchange their earthly lives for Paradise in service of God. *Muhakkima* probably came from the Arabic phrase *"la hukma illa li'llah"* ("judgement belongs to God alone"). Religious Studies scholar Adam Gaiser recently critiqued use of the term *khariji*, in part because of the negative connotations created by some of the more extreme offshoots of the movement. Instead, Gaiser uses *Muhakkima* or *shurat* as value neutral terms for the group as a whole, reserving Khariji for the more militant groups (such as the *Azariqa* and *Najdat*). I will continue to use *Khariji* only because it remains the most common term used by historians.

After Siffin, the *Khariji*s continued to oppose ʻAli. Over time, they developed the position that the caliphate should be held by the purest Muslim: the only criteria for identifying the true Imam was pious merit, not descent from the Prophet or ethnicity (a fairly radical proposition in the seventh century). Eventually, a *Khariji* assassinated 'Ali.

As they began organizing in Basra in Iraq in the late seventh century, the *Kharijis* formed four main sub-movements: the *Azariqa, Najdat, Sufriyya*, and *Ibadis*. The groups tended to split over questions of leadership as well as theological issues related to sin, apostasy, and whether or not it was permissible for *Kharijis* to live amongst non-*Kharijis*.[25] Most of these movements did not survive into the modern era. The *Azariqa* held the most extreme views, arguing that they could not live among non-*Kharijis* and that it was acceptable to execute Muslims who were not *Kharijis*. Their movement mostly disappeared after 699. The *Najdat* were mostly active in Arabia; their rebellion was suppressed in 693 but the group remained in existence for several centuries. Later, the *Sufriyya* appeared in Iraq and North Africa, surviving until the tenth century. The *Ibadis*, which were the most moderate of the offshoots, established states in North Africa and Oman and survive to this day.

Khariji movements succeeded in North Africa and Oman. *Khariji* rebels fled to North Africa in the early eighth century, taking refuge among the Berber population and inspiring a major anti-'Umayyad rebellion in 739–740. Within North Africa, *Sufriyya* and *Ibadi Khariji* groups competed for influence, especially around the city of Qayrawan. The *Ibadis* eventually established the Rustamid dynasty in Algeria in the 770s and survived until the early tenth century, when the Fatimids conquered their territory. The *Ibadis* also moved into Oman, establishing an Imamate there in the eighth century (and even briefly conquering Medina in 748). The *Ibadis* still constitute a majority of Oman's population, making up approximately seventy-five percent of the population there. They also sent missionaries into northeast Iran (Khurasan). The *Ibadis* reject the connection of their movement with the *Kharijis*, arguing that they opposed the more extreme *Khariji* doctrines even in the earliest period.

If you look up the *Khariji*s online, you will find a lot of commentary linking *Khariji* thought with twenty-first century terrorist movements such as ISIS and al-Qaeda because some of the more radical *Khariji* groups engaged in *takfir*, where they declared practising Muslims to be apostates for not following *Khariji* doctrines. This belief, however, was limited to the two more militant offshoots, the *Azariqa* and the *Najdat*. The *Ibadis* strongly oppose their association with the doctrine of *takfir*.

Khurramism

Muslim forces conquered the territories of Iran in the mid-seventh century and many Persians converted to Islam. Despite this, the mountainous regions of Iran often sheltered various types of religious movements that were considered heterodox. In addition to proto-Shi'i and *Khariji* activity there, Khurramism, which was a local religious movement that blended aspects of Islam with pre-existing practices and beliefs from Zoroastrianism, developed.

Khurramism was an outgrowth of Zoroastrianism. Before the Muslim conquest of Iran, Zoroastrianism was the official religion of the Sassanid dynasty, which ruled Iran from 224 to 651, but was also supported by all social classes within Iran. Based on the teachings of the Prophet Zoroaster, Zoroastrians preached an early form of monotheism where humans had free will to decide if they wanted to follow the one god. The Zoroastrian God was Ahura Mazda, the Wise Creator. Humans who chose not to follow Ahura Mazda fell under the sway of Angra Mainyu, a devil-like destructive spirit. Zoroastrian practice involved engaging in good deeds to avoid chaos. At the end of time, Zoroaster preached that Ahura Mazda would triumph over Angra Mainyu, leading to the end of time and a sort of Day of Judgment. Zoroastrianism can be dated back to approximately 1400–1200 BCE (although some scholars are only willing to date it back to the fifth century BCE), making it one of the world's oldest religions. It had a profound influence on the monotheistic faiths of the Middle East, influencing Judaism, Christianity, and Islam.

Scholars consider Khurramism a type of popular Zoroastrianism. While not a unified moment, it was believed to have begun as an ancient set of rural beliefs and practices that later became linked with a sixth-century Zoroastrian reform movement known as Mazdakism. Historian Patricia Crone argued that Khurramism should be considered a Zoroastrian-Muslim hybrid where Persian Muslims nativized Islamic beliefs and practices, combining them with existing popular beliefs. *Khurrami* Muslims saw themselves as Muslims, but rejected the Arab influence on the Prophet Muhammad's message.[26]

Many Persian Muslims supported the 'Abbasid revolution because they opposed the Arab superiority of the 'Umayyad dynasty. These Persian Muslims, already treated as outsiders by the Arab 'Umayyads, worshipped in their own mosques and were more than willing to join the 'Abbasid movement against the 'Umayyads. As mentioned above, the *Hashimiyya* movement, the proto-Shi'i movement which led to the rise of the 'Abbasids, recruited heavily in Persian territories. The *Hashimiyya* leader in Khurasan, who began the armed rebellion against the 'Umayyads, was known as Abu Muslim (a clear pseudonym: the name means "Father of a Muslim"). Abu Muslim was popular amongst the Persian *Khurramis*, some became Muslim because of his influence.

After the successful 'Abbasid revolution, the caliph assassinated Abu Muslim because he feared his popularity and influence in Iranian territory. Abu Muslim's death led to a dramatic rise in the number of *Khurrami* movements and their rejection of 'Abbasid Islam. Historians have identified at least seven separate *Khurrami* movements engaged in anti-'Abbasid organizing in the eighth and ninth centuries: such as the *Muslimiyya, Mubadiyya, Babakiyya, Rawandiyya, Rizamiyya, Barkukiyya*, and *Khidashiyya*. As Crone put it, "we should probably envisage the entire mountain range from Azerbaijan to Fars as dotted with [...] Khurrami cult societies."[27]

In a way, the above discussion of the proto-Shi'is, *Kharijis*, and *Khurramis* is a dramatic oversimplification. Specialists in these groups have long analysed and debated how these groups formed and their relationships with each other. Further, students do not usually learn much about these groups because most of them did not become dominant interpretations of Islam. But they are important because the prevalence and popularity of these movements reveals the degree to which, even in early Islam, Sunni Islam and urban Sunni religious scholars did not have a monopoly on defining Muslim faith and practice for most Muslims.

Notes

[22] Sean W. Anthony, "Heresiography," in *The Princeton Encyclopedia of Islamic Political Thought*, ed. Gerhard Bowering, Patricia Crone, and Mahan Mirza (Princeton: Princeton University Press, 2012).

[23] Roy P. Mottahedeh, "Pluralism and Islamic Traditions of Sectarian Divisions," in *Diversity and Pluralism in Islam: Historical and Contemporary Discourses Amongst Muslims*, ed. Zulfikar Hijri (London: I. B. Tauris, 2010), 32–34.

[24] William F. Tucker, *Mahdis and Millenarians: Shiite Extremists in Early Muslim Iraq* (Cambridge: Cambridge University Press, 2007).

[25] Adam Gaiser, *Shurat Legends, Ibadi Identities: Martyrdom, Asceticism, and the Making of an Early Islamic Community* (Columbia: University of South Carolina Press, 2016).

[26] Patricia Crone, *The Nativist Prophets of Early Islamic Iran: Rural Revolt and Local Zoroastrianism* (Cambridge: Cambridge University Press, 2012), 175–76.

[27] Ibid., 64.

Chapter 3

The Fatimids and Isma'ili Shi'ism in North Africa

The Fatimid caliphate arose out of an underground mission-ary movement which preached a proto-Isma'ili message. This movement culminated in the military conquest of North Africa in the tenth century. While details about the origins of the early Fatimid movement remain obscure, there was clear competition between different strands of proto-Isma'ilism. Scholars trace the portion of movement that founded the Fatimid caliphate to 'Abd Allah al-Mahdi (d. 934). Before the advent of the caliphate, the Fatimid Isma'ilis spent ten years engaged in armed rebellion against the 'Abbasid caliphate in parts of Iran, Iraq, Syria, Bahrain, Yemen, and North Africa. During this time, al-Mahdi made his way from Syria to North Africa. In 909, when al-Mahdi's forces conquered Qayrawan, the seat of the Aghlabid dynasty (r. 800–909), which ruled in the name of the 'Abbasids, al-Mahdi declared himself to be the first Fatimid caliph.

The Fatimids in North Africa sought to expand their rule with the eventual goal of overthrowing the 'Abbasid caliphate in Baghdad. During the caliphate of al-Mahdi and his son and successor al-Qa'im (d. 946), they attempted to conquer Egypt several times without success. During al-Qa'im's reign, the Fatimids also faced a prolonged rebellion by local *Ibadi Khar-iji* Berbers, which lasted from 943 to 947. The third Fatimid caliph, al-Mansur (d. 953), defeated this rebellion. His son and successor, al-Mu'izz (d. 975), successfully conquered Egypt and founded the new Fatimid imperial capital of Cairo to commemorate their success.

The Fatimids claimed descent from 'Ali and Fatima. But, despite taking Fatima as their namesake, they did not make their descent from 'Ali a central argument in their claim to authority. While later heresiographies accused the Fatimids of cursing the first three caliphs (Abu Bakr, 'Umar, and 'Uthman, remembered by Sunnis as the *Rashidun*) for usurping 'Ali's power, none of the tenth-century sources reported that any of the first four Fatimid caliphs publicly cursed the *Rashidun*.[28]

What might constitute Shi'i claims to authority would have still been in flux in the tenth century. After all, this period is the era when Shi'i identity was beginning to crystalize into distinct forms. But we would expect those claims to focus on the Imamate, descent from 'Ali and Fatima, and attacks on the *Rashidun* caliphs. Strikingly, these elements are not emphasized in Fatimid claims to authority. They did not make overtly Shi'i or Isma'ili claims to authority but used titles, architecture, and historical narratives to claim that they were legitimate *Muslim* rulers, not merely Shi'i leaders. Moreover, even Sunni religious scholars living under Fatimid rule did not predominately view the Fatimids through the lens of Shi'i identity. While Sunni religious scholars were sometimes critical, they accepted the Fatimids as legitimate Muslim rulers and did not focus their critiques on the Fatimids' Shi'i identity.

This chapter will analyse Fatimid claims to authority to rule and reactions to them from Sunni religious scholars in the tenth century. In this, we will focus on the early Fatimid dynasty—the period of the advent of the caliphate through the establishment of Cairo as their capital. From this, we can see that the Fatimids followed a similar trajectory to the 'Abbasids: arising out of an underground religious movement, their early claims for legitimacy rested on critiques of the 'Abbasids and their failure to follow the example of the Prophet (as the 'Abbasids had galvanized their revolution based on opposition to the 'Umayyads). Over time, however, the Fatimids adopted traditional medieval modes of articulating authority, copying the 'Abbasid model of rule in order to more directly compete with the rival caliphate.

The Fatimids were savvy communicators. They had organized an underground missionary movement that recruited supporters across the Middle East and carefully selected a moment and location to declare their caliphate where they thought they would succeed. When analysing their rhetoric, I argue that we can assume that they were aware of their audience and carefully planned how they would claim authority in a way that would be acceptable to the broadest possible audience.

Building on Local Opposition to the 'Abbasids

In their rhetoric, the Fatimids capitalized on discontent felt towards local leaders ruling in the name of the 'Abbasids. In North Africa, the 'Abbasids (and the 'Umayyads before them) had a contentious relationship with the local Berber population. The Berbers (today, this ethnic group prefers the term *Amazigh*, which means "free people") are an indigenous ethnolinguistic group of North Africa. While many Berbers converted to Islam during the seventh century, the 'Umayyads and the 'Abbasids struggled to exert effective direct control over the region. Muslim forces conquered North Africa in the seventh century, but this success was temporary. The 'Umayyads lost most of the territory during a series of major Berber revolts (740–743), after which several small Berber states ruled by tribal chieftains and *Khariji* Imams controlled most of western North Africa. The 'Abbasids still held some control, however, and when the Fatimids conquered Qayrawan in 909, they forced out the Aghlabids, the local Arab dynasty which ruled in the name of the 'Abbasid caliph in Baghdad.

In claiming their own right to rule, the Fatimids portrayed the Aghlabids—and through them the 'Abbasids—as unfit as either Muslims or rulers. In 957, Qadi al-Nu'man (d. 974), the first chief *qadi* (judge) of the Fatimids, completed *The Opening of the Mission* (*Kitab Iftitah al-Da'wa*), a Fatimid-sponsored history of the foundation of the caliphate. Medieval histories were written for multiple audiences. In part, they were composed for the rulers themselves: to create an official narrative of the dynasty and contextualize it within the longer scope of history. However, these types of stories could also be read by local scholars, missionaries, and storytellers and, via these groups, passed on to a more general public. Historical writing played a significant role in claiming legitimacy.

In his history, al-Nu'man portrayed the final Aghlabid ruler in North Africa, Ziyadat Allah (r. 903–909), as a debaucher who failed to uphold even the most basic tenets of Islam. He claimed that Ziyadat Allah had "committed forbidden acts and applied himself assiduously to pleasure and drinking wine" (147–48).[29] From what we can confirm from other histories of the Aghlabids, it appears that Ziyadat Allah made an excellent foil for the Fatimids: he came to power by having his own father assassinated and even ordering his assassins to bring him his father's head to prove that he was dead. Then, once in power, Ziyadat Allah executed the assassins and any of his own male relatives who might challenge his power in the future. According to al-Nu'man, even his own family condemned him: his grandfather had once imprisoned him "because of his corruption and committing fornication" (154).

Al-Nu'man argued implicitly that the Fatimids made better Muslim rulers than the 'Abbasids, often reminding his audience that Ziyadat Allah had a reputation for hypocrisy and was recognized as a poor example of a Sunni Muslim:

> [Ziyadat Allah] was called a Sunni. And he wrote on his banners: "Victory from God to the *amir* Ziyadat Allah b. 'Abd Allah, the follower of the *sunna* of the Prophet of God," and this despite his immorality, wantonness, corruption, and committing crimes against his father. So the people were not swayed by him and they didn't follow him. And it became known about him that he drank wine, which wasn't known in *Ifriqiya* [North Africa] before him. And he introduced singing and musical instruments, and gathered the people of entertainment, effeminate men, and jokers. He wouldn't stop drinking wine and was almost always to be seen drunk (155–56).

While al-Nu'man mentioned Ziyadat Allah's Sunni identity, he focused on his hypocrisy as a Sunni, not on attacks on him for being a Sunni. Al-Nu'man, writing approximately a generation after the fall of Ziyadat Allah, reminded local North Africans, both Sunnis and Shi'is who might remember his reign, that Ziyadat Allah was not remembered as a good Muslim leader. Thus, in an official history of their rise to power, the Fatimids favourably compared themselves with the Aghlabids. This claim did not even need to refer to the Fatimids' Shi'i identity but was based in their broader claim to be ideal Muslim rulers.

In addition to attacking Ziyadat Allah, the Fatimids also rhetorically linked the Aghlabids and the 'Abbasids in order to discredit the legitimacy of both. For example, al-Nu'man reported that the 'Abbasid caliph al-Muktafi (r. 902–908) sent a delegation to Ziyadat Allah, presenting him with gifts, robes of honour, and a letter from the caliph to be read aloud from mosques. In the letter, according to al-Nu'man, al-Muktafi praised Ziyadat Allah extensively:

> I have already told you of the situation of Ziyadat Allah b. 'Abd Allah in terms of friendship, sincerity, and adherence to the Commander of the Faithful [the 'Abbasid caliph], and pursuing his path, imitating his example, abiding by his obligation, following his oath, his good conduct, kindness to the subjects, and establishing justice [...]. Whoever's conduct follows the example of Ziyadat Allah, his relationship is certain, and his tie is close with the Commander of the Faithful (196).

Not only did the 'Abbasid caliph praise Ziyadat Allah, but he praised him as a good Muslim and a sincere friend. Further, al-Nu'man argued that the 'Abbasids *knew* that Ziyadat Allah was a poor Muslim. According to al-Nu'man, Ziyadat Allah tried to flee to Baghdad after he was ousted by the Fatimids. But the 'Abbasids denied him permission to enter the city due to his reputation for debauchery and wine-drinking (267). The 'Abbasids wanted Ziyadat Allah to remain in power over North Africa but would not let him enter their own capital city.

The Fatimids reinforced the message of Aghlabid and 'Abbasid hypocrisy in their speeches. In one of his *khutba*s, a type of speech given at the mosque during the community Friday prayer, the second Fatimid caliph al-Qa'im (d. 946) accused the subordinates of the 'Abbasid caliph of failing to follow even the basic rules of Islam:

> And yet among them [the 'Abbasids] a woman brings them wine from every valley and region on the backs of horses and in the bottoms of ships [...]. You have seen their governors of cities, how one of them mounts the wooden planks of the Prophet's *minbar* (pulpit) to preach to the people but does not preach to himself. Instead, he descends from that position and inquires of those in that land for male and female singers, *tunbur* [long-necked lute] and *'ud* [lute] players, thieves, short change artists, and shavers of weights so that those can be brought to serve him. God curses the unjust and prepares for them a blazing fire. That man is someone who neither commands the good nor prohibits the bad (89).[30]

Commanding the good and prohibiting the bad is considered a requirement upon all Muslims and, here, al-Qa'im accused the 'Abbasid caliph and his subordinates of failing to do both while breaking the Muslim prohibitions against wine, women, and song.[31] Not only that, but al-Qa'im accused the 'Abbasid officials who controlled the holy city of Medina, the city of the Prophet Muhammad's tomb, of preaching while patronizing (and thereby condoning) the activities of female singers, musicians, and thieves. The charge that they neither commanded the good nor forbade the wrong was also a pointed critique of the Malikis, a Sunni legal school popular in North Africa and the Fatimid capital, which particularly emphasized the importance of following this rule. It made a clear argument, directed at the religious scholars living under Fatimid rule, that the Fatimids acted as better Muslims than the 'Abbasids or the Aghlabids.

Al-Qa'im tried to show the hypocrisy of the 'Abbasids on more than one occasion, but he did not focus on sectarian identity in his attacks. During a speech in Alexandria, al-Qa'im said:

I observe the inhabitants of the cities; they pray against me in their mosques [...]. The lying apostate community, reneging on its intentions, deviating from the command of their Lord, suppose that it has been correct in what it claims about its caliphs whom they insist are the caliphs of the Lord of the worlds, such as a youth not yet mature, or like the boy lacking knowledge, or like the child who, according to their claim, governs Islam (88–89).

Al-Qa'im singled out the current 'Abbasid caliph, al-Muqtadir (r. 908–932), as the "youth not yet mature [...] who [...] governs Islam." Al-Qa'im built upon existing controversy surrounding al-Muqtadir, who became caliph when he was only thirteen years old; many considered him too young to rule and a puppet of his advisors. Despite the fact that al-Qa'im still did not call out the Abbasid caliph by name, his attack would have been clear to a tenth-century Muslim audience. He argued that the 'Abbasid caliph was invalid and failing to lead the Muslim community; thus, the Fatimids were the true leaders of Islam.

In addition to attacking their enemies, the Fatimids also compared themselves with the armies of the Prophet Muhammad, which conquered North Africa in the seventh century. This comparison made use of a well-known framework from existing histories of the seventh-century conquests.[32] Stories of those conquests were very popular among Muslim audiences and had several known tropes, or rhetorical devices, which the Fatimids adopted to describe their conquest of North Africa in the ninth century. Medieval historians did not have the same goals as modern historians: historical texts often served a didactic purpose, making an argument for how a society should view their own past. Thus, historians often related the stories of the seventh-century conquests as a cosmic battle of a poor but pious Muslim army confronting the extraordinarily wealthy but morally-corrupt powers of great antiquity. By portraying the conquests in this way, it implicitly argued that, when Muslim forces won despite overwhelming odds against them, God supported them. Using tropes from the conquest literature allowed the Fatimids, rhetorically, to place their own struggle in the context of the original Muslim conquests: the Fatimids were the Muslims and the Aghlabids were the non-Muslim armies of antiquity.

Fatimid historical writing also made use of these well-known tropes to portray themselves as heirs of the Prophet. For example, one common trope from the conquest narratives portrayed the wealthy Muslim enemies as trying to tempt the Muslim armies with gifts and wealth. Thus, the Fatimids depicted the Aghlabids as trying to use their tremendous wealth to ensnare the population of North Africa and defeat the righteous Fatimid armies. Al-Nuʿman's history of the Fatimid conquest depicted Ziyadat Allah as repeatedly passing out gold coins, weapons, and robes of honour to bribe his armies and the people of North Africa:

> [Ziyadat Allah] called to the towns by profusely giving gifts to the infantry and the cavalry and he sent parties of men to the chief towns and garrisons. He ordered the members of his family, all his courtiers, and his men to head out with him. A great army gathered to him. People came to him from everywhere to request gifts and he began to sit under a dome in Raqqada called the Dome of the Parade. Dinars were poured forth in front of him. The people of the towns were reviewed before him and he gave them gifts. If one passed him that pleased him, scoop by scoop he would pick up dinars with a plate in front of him that was wide enough for about fifty dinars. And he would give these to him. The news that he was giving [gifts] with a plate spread and people came to him from all directions (199).

Here, al-Nuʿman argued that no one followed Ziyadat Allah because he was a good Muslim ruler but because he bribed his people with money and supplies. Fatimid history frequently repeated these descriptions of Ziyadat Allah's attempts to buy the loyalty of the people of North Africa. But no matter how many times Ziyadat Allah distributed gold, his money could not overcome the piety of the Fatimids and their followers. This rhetorical argument may have resonated with a broader Muslim audience than only Ismaʿili Shiʿis. After all, the Fatimids were not making a sectarian argument for why they should hold power. Instead, they argued that their legitimacy was based in following the precepts of the Prophet Muhammad while the Aghlabids and the 'Abbasids had become corrupt.

Some early Fatimid rhetoric made fairly aggressive claims to authority, such as when al-Qa'im emphasized that the Muslim community had been led astray by their leaders, whom he likened to apostates and hypocrites. Arising out of the context of a revolutionary underground movement fighting the dominance of the 'Abbasid caliphate, this type of rhetoric does not seem unexpected. Significantly, however, even then, al-Qa-'im did not make *sectarian* appeals. He said that the 'Abbasid caliph was illegitimate—not because the 'Abbasids were not descendants of 'Ali and Fatima, but because the current caliph was too young and lacked knowledge. Al-Qa'im did not express his opposition to the 'Abbasids in ways that would be recognizably *Shi'i*. He even avoided attacking figures that would have alienated a non-Sunni audience, such as the first three caliphs who the Shi'is saw as illegitimate.

Rather than focusing on a specifically Shi'i or Isma'ili appeal to power, al-Qa'im blamed the leaders of the Muslim world for leading the community astray. He portrayed those leaders as hypocrites and bad Muslims, condemned to hell:

> Oh people, truly you have fallen into an iniquitous blindness and a dark blackness, overwhelmed by a calamity that carries you into another calamity; it has led you astray by its heretical delusions and overcome you with its pernicious atmosphere. You are floating in its misfortune, drowning in its ideology, its doors locked against you, its reasons become obscure, the guide-markers of your religion obliterated, the works of your prophet effaced, the abomination among you obvious. And the acceptable is with you extinct. Where is it you are headed? To the hellfire from which you cannot withdraw? Will you therefore be among those rewarded or those punished? (89–90)

Even in al-Qa'im's direct attacks where he named enemies of the Shi'is, he focused on attacking members of the 'Umayyad family who had failed to protect 'Ali and his family. This type of attack would have been familiar to a tenth-century audience because the 'Abbasids themselves had pioneered it. The 'Abbasids claimed that their own rise to power was a return to an idealized view of the first community under the Prophet and attacked the 'Umayyads for usurping power. Thus, al-Qa-'im, like the 'Abbasids themselves, harnessed existing hostility towards the 'Umayyads and respect for the family of the Prophet Muhammad.

Following the 'Abbasid Model

Even though the Fatimids attacked the 'Abbasids, they also adopted claims to legitimacy modelled on the 'Abbasids. The ways that the Fatimids chose to make these claims shows us how, during the tenth century, Muslim identity was not yet predominately organized around sectarianism. The third Fatimid caliph, al-Mansur, most obviously followed 'Abbasid precedents for claiming authority, evident in his choice of regnal name and in the Fatimid habit of capital building.

Al-Mansur's title itself can be read as a direct taunt against the 'Abbasids. His full regnal name was *al-Mansur billah*, which means "victory of God" in Arabic (for simplicity, I have been referring to the Fatimid caliphs by their official regnal names, not their birth names: al-Mansur's name was Abu Tahir Isma'il). Referring to himself as "victory of God" can be read as a not-so-subtle insult directed at the 'Abbasids: the Fatimids had been victorious in North Africa, conquering 'Abbasid territories. But, more significantly, it also clearly harkened back to the best-known holder of this title, the second 'Abbasid caliph al-Mansur (r. 754–775).

Choosing the second 'Abbasid caliph as a model was a potent strategic choice by the Fatimid al-Mansur. Both al-Mansurs served as early caliphs in a new dynasty which came to power after an underground revolutionary movement followed by local rebellions. The 'Abbasid al-Mansur took over shortly after the 'Abbasid revolution and fought rival claimants to the caliphate from within his own family and from proto-Shi'i movements. The Fatimid al-Mansur was the third

Fatimid caliph and, when he came to power, he faced a *Khariji* rebellion that had nearly conquered all of the Fatimid territory in North Africa. The 'Abbasid al-Mansur was the second 'Abbasid caliph, but is remembered as even more significant than his predecessor because he consolidated 'Abbasid power, established a stable bureaucracy based on a salaried army and an efficient system of taxation, and founded the new 'Abbasid capital city of Baghdad. The Fatimid al-Mansur's reign paralleled his 'Abbasid namesake's: after defeating local rebellions, he consolidated Fatimid power and founded a new capital city, *Mansuriyya*, named after himself. He is remembered as establishing the framework of the Fatimid caliphate that lasted until the twelfth century.

The two al-Mansurs also shared another significant parallel: both were remembered for their triumphant capital cities. Establishing capital cities represented a significant way that medieval dynasties claimed their authority to rule. They allowed a new ruler to showcase his victories and display his power, wealth, and prestige. The 'Abbasid capital, Baghdad, was the first Muslim capital city built from the ground up by a Muslim caliph. The 'Abbasid caliph al-Mansur ordered its construction in the eighth century. Similarly, the Fatimid caliph al-Mansur also built a capital city, *Mansuriyya*, which directly copied 'Abbasid Baghdad.

The 'Abbasids designed their capital city to challenge the 'Umayyads, who they had overthrown, and the Sassanids, the pre-Islamic Persian dynasty which had ruled over Iraq and Iran (and been conquered by the early Muslims). Baghdad was situated near the site of the former Sassanid capital, Ctesiphon. This location symbolically allowed the 'Abbasids to supplant the Sassanids and co-opt their power and prestige. They took the symbolic role of their capital seriously. For example, Baghdad had four gates, each looking out over a quadrant of 'Abbasid territory and representing 'Abbasid military victories: Iran/Central Asia, Mecca, Syria, and southern Iraq. We do not know the origins of all four gates, but the gate facing Iran (known as the Khurasan Gate) was constructed by the Byzantine Empire and taken from Syria. The 'Umayyads made the gate facing Mecca (known as the Kufa Gate).

'Abbasid Baghdad also possessed a striking design that highlighted its symbolic significance as the caliphal capital. It was created as a royal city, where the caliph lived with his family, military, and the 'Abbasid bureaucracy, separate from the regular population over whom he ruled. The city was designed to showcase the power and prestige of the caliph: composed with a circular plan, the caliph's palace stood in the centre, literally at the crossroads of the routes that led from the four main city gates. This circular model had been adopted from the pre-Islamic Sassanids who had built circular cities to serve as symbolic representations of their view of the universe: all roads leading to the ruler who stood at the centre.[33] The caliph's palace also boasted an impressive dome to mark its significance. This design also copied other capitals: the Byzantine and Sassanid emperors had both used domed palaces and churches to show their closeness to the powers of heaven. Thus, the domed 'Abbasid palace in the centre of their imperial city built to represent the world symbolically represented the 'Abbasid view of themselves as dominating the crossroads of the world.

The Fatimids copied Baghdad directly. The Fatimids had made a bit of a hobby of establishing new capitals; *Mansuriyya* was only one of the new Fatimid capitals established in the first seventy years of Fatimid rule. Of the first four Fatimid caliphs, only al-Qa'im did not build a capital city of his own. All three Fatimid capitals followed the models of 'Abbasid Baghdad, which, in turn, had followed pre-Islamic precedents. Cairo was the last and best-known of the Fatimid capitals and the fourth Fatimid caliph, al-Mu'izz, built it to mimic and surpass 'Abbasid Baghdad. Like *Mansuriyya*, the name of al-Mu'izz's capital, *al-Qahira* in Arabic, meant "The Victorious" and commemorated the Fatimid victory over Egypt.

Like Baghdad, Cairo was designed as a round city with four gates, with roads that symbolically divided the city into the four corners of the world. Cairo was originally called *Mansuriyya*, after the capital city built by al-Mansur in North

Africa. Later sources recount that the caliph al-Mu'izz himself drew the plan for the palace; while this claim seems unlikely, it suggests the central significance of the city's plan to the Fatimid caliph's project of embodying the sacred power of the caliphate.

The Fatimids directly followed 'Abbasid precedents for claiming authority. Fatimid victory in Egypt and the foundation of Cairo represented a great triumph for the Fatimid caliphs, both literally and figuratively, against their rivals. Cairo, the capital they built, soaked in spiritual meaning: the caliph al-Mu'izz carried the coffins of his ancestors, the first three Fatimid caliphs, with him to Cairo in order to re-inter their bodies in the new Fatimid capital. The palace city of Cairo housed the palaces of the caliph and his successor, the renowned Fatimid library, and the new Fatimid university, al-Azhar, where the chief Fatimid missionaries delivered lectures.

Establishing Order and Enforcing Islamic Law

Finally, the Fatimids portrayed themselves as a return to the order of the Prophet Muhammad by following expectations of a Muslim audience in addition to emphasizing their excellent administration of local territories and their enforcement of Islamic law. These appeals focused on emphasizing the ways that the Fatimids made ideal Muslim rulers, not on their sectarian identity.

In public religious speeches, the Fatimids adapted their speeches to the style that would be expected by a broad Muslim audience, not just Shi'i Muslims. In the medieval Islamic state, the *khutba*, the sermon given during the communal prayer on Friday, served as one of the key ceremonies that symbolized the caliph's role as the leader of the Muslim community. Tahera Qutbuddin, in "*Khutba*: The Evolution of Early Arabic Oration," analysed *khutba*s, their style, and how Muslim audiences developed expectations about the structure and style of this speech.[34] Analysing the surviving Fatimid *khutba*s and how they changed over time shows that the Fatimids adapted their *khutba*s to the existing expectations of a Muslim audience.

According to Qutbuddin, the structure of the *khutba* developed over time and, by the tenth century, had a fairly consistent framework with at least six formulaic elements. It began with a exaltation of God (*tahmid*), followed by the testimony of faith (*shahada*), the glorification of God (*subhana*), an entreaty for God's aid (*isti'ana*), and the invocation of blessings on the Prophet Muhammad (*salawat*). It ended with a prayer for forgiveness, which usually involved the phrase "I say these words and beg forgiveness from God for myself and for all believing men and women" (205–6).

The format of the Fatimid *khutba*s changed dramatically in the first thirty years of the Fatimid rule. No *khutba*s survived from al-Mahdi's reign, but *khutba*s from al-Qa'im do not follow the expected formula in any way. Al-Mansur and al-Mu'izz's *khutba*s, however, adhered much more closely to patterns of the 'Abbasid *khutba*, conforming to audience expectations for the speech. We can see this in al-Mansur's *khutba*s. He began with the traditional exultation of God (*tahmid*), saying: "In the name of God, the Merciful, the Compassionate. Praise be to God who created the heavens and the earth, and made the darkness and the light," then stated the Muslim testament of faith (*shahada*), "I bear witness that there is no god but God, alone, without associate, and I testify that Muhammad was His servant and His chosen messenger." Then, he made an invocation of blessings upon the Prophet (*salawat*), reciting, "God bless him among those who were first and those who were later. [Bless also] his family, the pure and the chaste, the chosen legatees, the most distinguished rightly guided ones." We can see a nod to al-Mansur's Shi'ism in this section, as he mentions the family of the Prophet and calls them the "chosen legatees" (13–15), which was a fairly direct reference to the Imams. While these comments can be considered to be expressing a Shi'i orientation, all Muslims revered the family of the Prophet.

We can see how the Fatimid *khutba*s followed the expected pattern of 'Abbasid *khutba*s most clearly in how they ended.

Again, there was a clear shift from the time of al-Qa'im to al-Mansur. As mentioned above, Muslims would expect the *khutba* to end with a prayer for forgiveness, which, according to Qutbuddin, usually incorporated the phrase "I say these words and beg forgiveness from God for myself and for all believing men and women" (205). The first *khutba* of al-Qa'im contained no such prayer for forgiveness, but, rather, ended with an attack on the 'Umayyads. Al-Qa'im's second *khutba* also ended with an attack on enemies of the state. Beginning with al-Mansur, however, the Fatimid *khutba*s adopted the prayer for forgiveness at the end of their speeches. They did not follow the exact pattern of 'Abbasid *khutba*s, but the similarity is evident; the Fatimid *khutba*s nearly always used phrasing very close to this: "O God, forgive the believers, male and female, and the Muslims, men and women, the living among them and the dead" (17). The prayer for forgiveness, with minor differences in phrasing, is found in four of al-Mansur's six surviving *khutba*s. It is also found in the two surviving *khutba*s from al-Muʻizz. Conforming more directly to existing formulas for *khutba*s allowed the Fatimid caliphs to embody the authority of the 'Abbasid caliphs and conform to audience expectations.

Fatimid histories also argued that God supported al-Mahdi, the first Fatimid caliph. They did this rhetorically by showing how, when al-Mahdi travelled to North Africa to establish his caliphate, he evaded capture at every step because he had God's protection. For example, in a history of the Fatimid caliphate written by Jaʻfar al-Hajib (fl. tenth century), who accompanied al-Mahdi on his journey from Syria to North Africa, he presented al-Mahdi as narrowly avoiding capture by the 'Abbasid army in Syria and avoiding discovery on the Mediterranean coast because he was warned by a local missionary. In addition, God's support was often shown as support by 'Abbasid officials, who Fatimid histories presented as recognizing the legitimacy of al-Mahdi. In several occasions, 'Abbasid officials either looked the other way or refused direct orders to arrest al-Mahdi (110–12).[35]

Jaʻfar also presented al-Mahdi as narrowly avoiding capture because of things that looked like chance but were always presented as evidence of God's support: al-Mahdi was saved because he could predict what would happen and because his supporters displayed unwavering loyalty. For example, even though the 'Abbasids searched for al-Mahdi, he avoided capture in North Africa because, when stopped, he was not recognized (115). His followers refused to betray him: one of his missionaries was captured by would not reveal al-Mahdi's whereabouts (116). Further, the histories implied on multiple occasions that al-Mahdi foresaw the future, making decisions that his supporters later saw as having helped them avoid capture (118–19).

Fatimid-sponsored histories emphasized how they followed the tradition of the Prophet in a way that had been abandoned by local 'Abbasid rulers. In speeches given by the Fatimid caliphs, they emphasized their desire to closely follow the dictates of Islamic law while Fatimid histories portrayed local 'Abbasid rulers as hypocrites and violators of Islamic law. In these, they also often chose to emphasize aspects of religious law that would have been fully compatible with Sunni law. For example, al-Nu'man emphasized how al-Qa'im avoided breaking the precepts of Islamic law, while castigating the armies of other local Muslim rulers for their failure to follow religious law:

> O Jawhar, do not eat any meat other than the permissible meat that we provide for you from our kitchen, for all that is sold in the markets of the army is foul, because the soldiers commit impermissible acts and have found ways to perpetrate plunder.[36]

The implication was that non-Fatimid Muslim soldiers failed to follow Islamic law. A biography of the Fatimid caliphs included a collection of letters written by the caliphs themselves. These letters emphasized the Fatimids' attempts to fulfil the highest expectations of a Muslim ruler by maintaining efficient and effective administration of their territory. They include letters from al-Mansur ordering the punishment of local officials who did not protect caravans, allowed fraud, embezzled money from taxes, or drank alcohol. The letters also showed how the Fatimid caliphs tried to follow the best practices of a Muslim ruler: making regular inspections of coinage, arbitrating disputes, and respecting the sanctity of mosques. In other words, Fatimid official correspondence, predominately about conducting the business of an Islamic state, presented the Fatimids as very concerned with following the best norms for the behaviour of Muslim leaders.

Reactions to the Fatimids

Often, because of the paucity of surviving sources, when historians examine the history of the Fatimids they will incorporate sources from the tenth through fourteenth centuries (and sometimes later). I argue that narrative sources from after the eleventh century present an overtly sectarian view of the Fatimids (and Buyids) while, if we look at exclusively contemporary tenth-century sources, we can see a distinct difference in how Shi'i dynasties were presented, even in sources written by Sunni religious scholars. In this section, we will examine contemporary reactions to the Fatimids. In the conclusion, we will address how later sources focus on the sectarian identity of the Fatimids.

The first two Fatimid caliphs, al-Mahdi and al-Qa'im, did not attempt to impose Isma'ili Shi'ism on the people of North Africa, but they placed greater emphasis on their roles as the leaders of a millenarian movement anticipating the end of the world and the Day of Judgement. Thus, al-Mahdi outlawed the teaching of Sunni doctrine and the issuance of Sunni legal decisions (*fatwas*). Not unsurprisingly, this caused Sunni opposition. However, while local Sunnis opposed the Fatimid takeover of North Africa at first, their opposition evaporated after they were able to secure jobs with the Fatimid administration. None of the surviving tenth-century Sunni accounts of Fatimid rule presented their opposition as based in sectarian hostility.

The Fatimid caliphs after al-Qa'im distanced themselves from this Shi'i millenarianism, embracing their status as Muslim caliphs ruling over a diverse population of both Muslims and non-Muslims. Al-Mansur, the third Fatimid caliph, reversed al-Mahdi's official opposition to Sunni doctrine and teachings and appointed some Maliki Sunnis to government posts. Once al-Mansur had reversed this anti-Sunni policy, Sunni Maliki opposition diminished significantly. It seems that the source of the Sunni Maliki opposition to the Shi'i Fatimids was not general sectarian hostility but opposition to the very specific threat to the economic livelihood and political power of Sunni Maliki religious scholars living under Shi'i Fatimid rule.

Three accounts of life in Fatimid North Africa written by Maliki Sunni scholars who lived under Fatimid rule survive: Al-Khushani (d. 981) was a Sunni Maliki who lived in Qayrawan when the Fatimids conquered the city. In 923, he left Qayrawan and resettled in Spain where he served at the court of the Sunni 'Umayyad dynasty. We may read it as significant that al-Khusani spent fourteen years living in Fatimid territory before he resettled in Spain. Ibn Abi Zayd al-Qayrawani (922–996) was a Sunni Maliki who also lived under Fatimid rule. He was the head of the Sunni Maliki school of jurisprudence in Qayrawan, the first Fatimid capital, and continued to teach, deliver religious rulings, and write about Sunni Maliki religious law. 'Arib b. Sa'd (d. ca. 980) was a Sunni Maliki who lived in Sunni 'Umayyad Spain, so he was not living under the power of the Fatimids. Overall, they portrayed their opposition to Shi'i Fatimid rule as predominately limited to the period of the first two Fatimid caliphs, al-Mahdi and al-Qa'im, who ruled from 909 to 946. Further, while they criticized some Shi'i beliefs and practices, these contemporary Sunni authors focused their hostility on conflicts and competition between the two main local Sunni groups, the Hanafis and the Malikis. In the tenth century, the different schools of Sunni jurisprudence were still in fierce competition.

Obviously, local Sunni religious scholars criticized Shi'i faith and practice. Al-Qayrawani, the leader of the Sunni Malikis under Fatimid rule, included the Shi'is among his list of the Muslims who had erred. He also sometimes referred to them as *Rafida*, a common medieval slur for Shi'is that meant deserter or defector and referred to the Sunni belief that the

Shi'is had rejected the rule of the Prophet's legitimate successors.[37] Al-Qayrawani published a manual of religious law
while he lived under Fatimid rule. In this manual, he did not
openly criticize Fatimid religious policies (which may have
been dangerous for him while living under Fatimid authority), but he did criticize some Shi'i positions. For example,
he emphasized that the best of the Muslims were Abu Bakr,
'Umar, and 'Uthman, *followed by* 'Ali, and argued that Muslims
should not prefer one of the first four caliphs over another.
For medieval Muslims, this assertion would be a clear rebut-
tal to the Shi'i belief that 'Ali was the only legitimate leader
amongst the first four caliphs. Al-Qayrawani also used his
religious manual to explain significant Sunni practices, often
ones that conflicted with official Fatimid religious policy,
such as the proper format of the call to prayer, the benefit of
additional prayers during Ramadan (*tarawih*), and the Sunni
method for dating the end of the Ramadan fast.

However, despite differences in practice, it also seems
evident that Sunnis such as al-Qayrawani considered the
Fatimids to be legitimate Muslim rulers. The question of
whether or not Muslims could live under non-Muslim rule was
a contentious issue in tenth-century Sunni discourse. Yet the
Sunni al-Qayrawani argued that Muslims may *not* oppose a
Muslim ruler for being oppressive or unjust. Rather, al-Qayrawani said that Muslims were even required to fight for
an unjust Muslim ruler. He devoted an entire section of his
religious manual to crimes against Islam, but these sections
never mentioned anything related to Shi'ism or Shi'i practices
associated with the Fatimids. It is clear that, while al-Qayrawani disagreed with Shi'i practices, he did not consider
the Fatimids to be un-Islamic.

The Malikis had a closer relationship with the local 'Abbasid dynasty which the Fatimids defeated. Thus, after the
Fatimid conquest, their competitors, the local Hanafis, were
often more willing to work with the Fatimids, increasing local
Maliki-Hanafi competition. According to a biographical dictionary written by al-Khushani, a Sunni Maliki scholar who spent
fourteen years living under Fatimid rule, several Sunni reli-

gious scholars in Qayrawan converted to Isma'ili Shi'ism in order to serve the Fatimid state, often as religious judges.[38] While some Maliki Sunnis converted, most of the Sunni converts came from the ranks of the Hanafis.

Even when there was actual persecution of Sunnis by the Shi'i Fatimids, the contemporary Sunni sources tended to blame their Sunni competitors. For example, in 909, after Fatimid forces conquered Qayrawan but before al-Mahdi had arrived, the acting leader of the Fatimids in Qayrawan publicly executed two Maliki scholars for making anti-Shi'i proclamations. However, rather than use this incident to emphasize Fatimid anti-Sunni activity (as it tends to get used in later sources), the contemporary Sunni Maliki sources blamed the Hanafis, saying that Hanafi attacks on the Malikis had led to their execution by the Fatimids. Further, the two contemporary Sunni Maliki accounts were written by Sunni religious scholars who had moved into Sunni 'Umayyad Spain, making it unlikely that their portrayals were influenced by fear of Fatimid reprisals.

Fatimid claims to legitimacy were nuanced and, often, followed models from the 'Abbasids themselves. These claims were not based in the Fatimids' Shi'i identity but in broader appeals to a wide variety of Muslims. The later Fatimids in Cairo, however, made more recognizably Shi'i claims to authority but always sought to appeal to a broad contingency of the people they ruled. While this chapter only examined the early Fatimid caliphate, Paula Sanders, in *Ritual, Politics, and the City in Fatimid Cairo*,[39] reconstructed Fatimid political culture of the eleventh and twelfth centuries from its court rituals. She argued that the Fatimids used ritual and public festivals in Cairo to appeal to a diverse non-Isma'ili and non-Muslim population. Irene Bierman's *Writing Signs: The Fatimid Public Text*,[40] also analysed how the Fatimids addressed multiple audiences in the eleventh and twelfth centuries, arguing that the Fatimids carefully balanced claims to legitimacy as Muslim caliphs and Shi'i Imams.

Notes

[28] We do know that at least one later Fatimid caliph, al-Hakim (d. 1021), did allow the public cursing of the first three caliphs. This, in part, shows how the Fatimids sectarianized their rhetoric over time.

[29] I will be citing from this edition: Qadi al-Nuʿman, *Kitab Iftitah al-Daʿwa* (Tunis: al-Sharikah al-Tunisiyah lil-Tawziʿa, 1975).

[30] When citing the *khutbas* of Fatimid caliphs, I will draw them from *Orations of the Fatimid Caliphs: Festival Sermons of the Ismaili Imams*, ed. and trans. Paul E. Walker (London: I. B. Tauris, 2009).

[31] For a more extensive discussion of the importance of the state's role in "forbidding wrong" as a significant means of constructing its own legitimacy, especially in sectarian contexts, see Michael Cook, *Forbidding Wrong in Islam* (Cambridge: Cambridge University Press, 2003), 65–72.

[32] Such as conquest stories told by Ibn ʿAbd al-Hakam (d. 871), Ibn Aʿtham (d. 926), and al-Tabari (d. 923). For more information on conquest literature and its tropes, see Thomas Sizgorich, "Do Prophets Come with a Sword?," *The American Historical Review* 112, no. 4 (October 2007), 993–1015.

[33] This argument is best made in Charles Wendell's "Baghdad, Imago Mundi and Other Foundation-Lore," *IJMES* (*International Journal of Middle East Studies*) 2, no. 2 (April 1971), 99–128.

[34] Tahera Qutbuddin, "Khutba: The Evolution of Early Arabic Oration," in *Classical Arabic Humanities in Their Own Terms: Festschrift for Wolfhart Heinrichs*, ed. Beatrice Gruendler and Michael Cooperson (Leiden: Brill, 2008), 176–273.

[35] For Jaʿfar's text, I will be citing from "Sirat Jaʿfar," in *Bulletin of The Faculty of Arts of the University of Egypt* 4, no. 2 (December 1936). Translations from the *Sirat Jaʿfar* are my own.

[36] *Sirat al-Ustadh Jawdhar*, 32. Hamid Haji translated the *Sirat al-Ustadh Jawdhar* as *Inside the Immaculate Portal* (London: I. B. Tauris, 2012) and, in this chapter, I am using his translations.

[37] I will be citing Ibn Abi Zayd al-Qayrawani's *Kitab al-Jamiʿ*, translated as *A Madinan View on the Sunnah, Courtesy, Wisdom, Battles, and History*, Abdassamad Clarke, ed. (London: Ta-Ha, 1999), 17–18. Al-Qayrawani also wrote a treatise on Islamic law, *al-Risala*, ed. Mahmoud Matraji (Beirut: Dar El-Fikr, 1994).

[38] Al-Khushani wrote a biographical dictionary of Sunni religious scholars: *Akhbar al-fuqaha wa al-muhaddithun* (Madrid: al-Majlis al-Aʿla lil-Abhath al-ʿIlmyah, Mahad li-Taʿawwun maʿa al-ʿAlam al-ʿArab, 1992).

[39] Paula Sanders, *Ritual, Politics, and the City in Fatimid Cairo* (Albany: State University of New York Press, 1994).

[40] Irene Bierman, *Writing Signs: The Fatimid Public Text* (Berkeley: University of California Press, 1998).

Chapter 4

The Buyids and Shiʿism in Baghdad

Like the Fatimids, the Buyids did not make Shiʿi claims to authority but modelled themselves on the expectations of a medieval Muslim audience. They rose to power within a generation of the Fatimids, taking control over ʿAbbasid Baghdad in 945. Like the Fatimids, the Buyids identified as Shiʿi. However, the Buyids did not come to power out of a Shiʿi revolutionary movement. The Buyids served as mercenaries for local Muslim dynasties in the mountains of northern Iran where many people had been converted to Islam by Zaydi missionaries. The Buyids tend to be best known in history for conquering the ʿAbbasid capital of Baghdad and holding the caliph hostage. Despite this fact, when we analyse Buyid rhetoric about their own legitimacy, they did not prioritize their Shiʿism. As non-Arab converts to Islam, they could not claim the caliphate nor the Imamate. Thus, they made diverse claims to legitimacy that do not fit neatly into conceptual categories that we typically use to define ethnic and religious identity in this era. Instead, we can see the Buyids as examples of the shifting nature of Muslim identity during this pivotal period in Islamic history when more of the peoples of the Middle East were converting to Islam.

The Buyids held power in Baghdad from 945–1055 and the most famous and powerful Buyid ruler, ʿAdud al-Dawla (d. 983), took over Baghdad in 979 and was proclaimed the *Amir al-Umara*, prince of princes, by the ʿAbbasid caliph. If we wanted a figure who embodied the tenth-century Islamic world—one which was only just becoming predominately Muslim and dealing with the influx of converts with a motley assortment of pre-Islamic identities—'Adud al-Dawla was it. He was a second-generation Muslim from a Persianate background. He was from a region of northern Iran called the Daylam. While part of Iran today, the Daylamites had a reputation as backward but skilled mercenaries; the proper Persians of the cities would not have considered the Daylamites to be Persian. While 'Adud al-Dawla's father was a powerful but uneducated military leader who probably did not read or speak Arabic,[41] 'Adud al-Dawla was educated in both Persian and Arabic by the skilled advisors of his father and uncle.

At the height of Buyid power, they ruled large portions of what is now Iraq and western Iran. In the west, they controlled parts of eastern Syria, although they competed with several other regional powers for those territories. Overall, Buyid power was most secure in the territories conquered by the founding three brothers of the Buyid triumvirate:[42] Rayy, an Iranian city near today's Tehran, located just outside of the Daylam; Shiraz, the capital of Fars province in the south, and Baghdad, the capital of the 'Abbasid caliphate, in modern Iraq. Daylam, Fars, and Iraq, however, were very different contexts: the populations of these areas had vastly different experiences with the Muslim conquests and, later, 'Abbasid rule.

This chapter will analyse Buyid claims to authority during the leadership of 'Adud al-Dawla as well as local reactions to the Buyids in Baghdad. The Buyids claimed complex forms of legitimacy and authority out of identities that, before their era, would have seemed completely incompatible. The Buyids were the first non-Arab, Shi'i dynasty to conquer Baghdad after the rise of Islam, but their appeals to authority do not fit neatly into categories of Persian or Shi'i. Instead, the Buyids blended ideas from pre-Islamic Persian kingship with Arabic and Islamic history and, even though they were Shi'i, they did not base their claims to power on sectarianism. The Buyid success in creating these hybrid forms of legitimacy revealed how they were not defined by their sectarian identity and, in local reactions to the Buyids, we can see how they were not primarily viewed through the lens of sectarianism.

Redefining Buyid Ethnicity

As non-Arabs, the Buyids could not claim descent from the Prophet Muhammad; thus, they could not claim the Imamate or the caliphate because both of those claims were based in descent from the Prophet. The Buyids originated in the Daylam, mountainous highlands of Iran just south of the Caspian Sea. The Daylamites had converted to Islam relatively late and were considered to be backwards and warlike, especially by urban Persians. In their attempts to establish their authority to lead the entire Islamic world, the Buyids distanced themselves from their Daylamite origins, adopted both Arab and elite Persian roots, and claimed descent from the pre-Islamic Sassanid kings.

In order to appeal to a broader ethnic audience, the Buyids attempted to create a history where the Daylamites could claim both Arab and Persian roots. First, they alleged that the Daylamites had an undiscovered Arab heritage. 'Adud al-Dawla sponsored a history written by Abu Ishaq al-Sabi which linked the Daylamites with a long-lost arm of an Arab tribe from Oman called the *Banu Dhabba*. According to this history, the *Banu Dhabba* had lived in Daylam from ancient times and maintained close relations with local Persians.[43] Calling the *Banu Dhabba* "the strongest and bravest Arabs," the Buyid history claimed that the Persians of Daylam intermarried with the *Banu Dhabba* to create a group of Daylamites of mixed ethnic heritage. Furthermore, al-Sabi avowed that the Arabs and Persians in the Daylam "blended together and began to resemble each other. Today, there is no difference between them in language, characteristics, morals, or customs." The emphasis on the early mixing of Arabs and Persians in the Daylam provided 'Adud al-Dawla with a hybrid Arab-Persian identity that also revitalized the reputation of the Daylamites, who had been described as "crude and unruly warrior bands [...] viewed with aversion and hatred by the more civilized population of the countries they invaded."

Long before 'Adud al-Dawla sponsored histories claiming descent from an Arab tribe, he had patronized one of the most famous Arab poets, al-Mutanabbi (d. 965), to write panegyric in his name. As Samer Ali has argued in *Arabic Literary Salons in the Islamic Middle Ages,* panegyric played a significant role in justifying the authority and privilege of a ruler in medieval Islamic society. The ruler's claim to authority was rooted in mythic precedents and, as such, required the development and maintenance of a mythology to display the king's mythic role. Praise hymns by poets let kings build their image and counter rivals. Susanne Pinckney Stetkevych, in *The Poetics of Islamic Legitimacy,* argued that medieval rulers used pan- egyric as a tool to spin military and political success into "the myth of ideology of legitimate rule" (180). The relationship between poet and patron can be seen as fairly mercenary. After all, the patron paid the poet for his panegyric. However, panegyric played a significant role in medieval Arabic society by extolling the virtues of kingship and reminding the public of the ruler's duties.

Al-Mutanabbi used his poetry to emphasize 'Adud al-Daw- la's Persianness but also make sense of this Persianness for an Arab audience. Al-Mutanabbi dedicated a poem called "The Gap of Bavvan" to 'Adud al-Dawla. In this poem, he uses many common symbols of Persian nobility, such as the lion and the sun, to describe 'Adud al-Dawla and his two sons:

> Never before have I seen two sturdy lion cubs
> Like his ['Adud al-Dawla's] two cubs swift as two colts
> More strongly contesting nobility of origins
> Or more like a noble father in appearance.
> (lines 37–38)

And then:

> You ['Adud al-Dawla] were the sun dazzling every eye
> So how now can two others shine?
> May they live the life of the two moons
> Giving life by their light and not envious of each
> other. (lines 42–43)[44]

It is not surprising that al-Mutanabbi used the lion and the sun, common symbols of Persian sovereignty, to describe

'Adud al-Dawla and his sons. But al-Mutanabbi also tries to make sense of 'Adud al-Dawla for an Arab audience.

"The Gap of Bavvan" deployed themes of discomfort between Arab and Persian culture but also portrayed 'Adud al-Dawla as the leader who could bring the two cultures together. Bavvan, a glade that al-Mutanabbi passed through in southeastern Iran, was known as a place of great natural beauty. In this environment, al-Mutanabbi expressed his feelings of alienation as an Arab traveller in a Persian land:

> But an Arab man there is
> A stranger in face, hand, and tongue
> Playgrounds to jinn, if Solomon roamed there
> He would take along an interpreter.
>
> (lines 2–3)[45]

Margaret Larkin, in *Al-Mutanabbi: Voice of the 'Abbasid Poetic Ideal*, interpreted this poem as portraying a "clear tension between Arab and Persian culture, which results in verses that sometimes verge on being disrespectful to the latter" (89). As an Arab, al-Mutanabbi expressed isolation in Persian territory. When he referred to Solomon's need of an interpreter in Persia, he alluded to a Qur'anic verse that described Solomon's ability to understand all the languages of the world and even speak to *jinn* (Qur'an 27: 16–17). Al-Mutanabbi felt that he needed assistance to understand this foreign environment. He compared how he felt in Persia with how he would feel in Damascus, Arab territory:

> If this were Damascus, my reins would be diverted
> By someone with kettles white as china, skilled at
> making *tharid* stew
> Who uses aloe wood to kindle a fire for guests,
> Whose smoke is fragrant with perfume
> You dwell with him with a brave heart
> And depart from him with a timorous one.
>
> (lines 10–12)

Al-Mutanabbi described scenes of Arab hospitality in Damascus. According to Larkin, "kettles white as china" served as a metaphor for a generous man (91). In *Politics, Gender, and the Islamic Past,* Denise Spellberg noted that many early and medieval Muslim sources mentioned that *tharid* stew was the Prophet Muhammad's favourite meal (162). Thus, mentioning *tharid* stew brought together Arabic and Islamic imagery. Al-Mutanabbi felt comfortable in Arab Damascus and feared leaving to enter Persia.

Al-Mutanabbi spent most of the poem expressing his discomfort in a Persian environment but, at the end of the poem, described how ʿAdud al-Dawla brought him comfort there:

> I said: When I see Abu Shujaʿ [ʿAdud al-Dawla's given name]
> I forget about everyone else and this place
> For people and the world are [but] a road
> To one who has no match among men.
>
> (lines 19–20)

Larkin argued that these lines were rendered more powerful by the fact that al-Mutanabbi spent the eighteen lines before them emphasizing his alienation.

Finally, al-Mutanabbi ended with the line, "I trained myself on poetry on them, just as one first learns to charge with a lance that has no point" (line 21). Here, al-Mutanabbi stressed ʿAdud al-Dawla's superiority to his other patrons. This was significant because al-Mutanabbi's best known patron was Sayf al-Dawla (d. 967), the Hamdanid ruler of Aleppo, whom he often portrayed as an ideal Muslim ruler. Claiming that ʿAdud al-Dawla surpassed all his other patrons emphasized the point that even Arabs should see him as an ideal.

Claiming Sassanid Kingship

Once he had established the Daylamites' heritage as Arabo-Persian, ʿAdud al-Dawla then announced that he was a descendant of the pre-Islamic Sassanid dynasty and adopted the title *Shahanshah*, "king of kings"; the Persian Sassanids took the title after they conquered and united Iran. This title allowed ʿAdud al-Dawla to claim to be of the same powerful lineage as the dynasty who had united and ruled Iran before the Muslim conquests. In addition, when 'Adud al-Dawla took this title, he also professed his descent from a particular Sassanid shah: Bahram Gur (d. 438).

The choice of Bahram Gur as his ancestor provided 'Adud al-Dawla with another opportunity to blend Arab and Persian heritage. Bahram Gur served as a significant symbol of harmony between Arabs and Persians. As a boy, Bahram Gur's father, the Sassanid shah, sent him to be raised at the court of al-Mundhir I (r. ca. 418–452), who ruled the Arab Lakhmids in southern Iraq. The Lakhmid capital was located in Hira, west of the Euphrates, not far from where Baghdad would later be established. When Bahram Gur's father died, his older brother (and the heir to the Sassanid throne) was assassinated and his royal power usurped. Bahram Gur, however, returned to his capital with an Arab army and retook the Sassanid throne. Claiming Bahram Gur as his ancestor allowed 'Adud al-Dawla to position himself as a figure who brought together the Arab and Persian traditions.

Bahram Gur made an ideal choice of ancestor for 'Adud al-Dawla because he was also quite a popular figure in tenth-century Baghdad. A famous medieval Islamic history, al-Tabari's *History of Prophets and Kings*, related Bahram Gur's life in extensive detail. According to al-Tabari (d. 923), three nurses had raised (and breastfed) Bahram Gur while he was with the Arab Lakhmids: two Arabs, and one Persian. Later participation of both Arab and Persian women in raising Bahram Gur was considered a sign of both nations' contribution to his greatness. When the Lakhmids helped Bahram Gur win back his throne, al-Tabari presented this aid as an act of unselfish assistance that was rewarded when Islamic forces won control over Persia. Bahram Gur was, thus, an important symbol of Persian-Arab cooperation.

In addition to Bahram Gur's individual attributes, 'Adud al-Dawla's claim of descent from the Sassanids also allowed him to build his legitimacy on their authority. He began using the title *Shahanshah* and made a ceremonial visit to the city of Persepolis, the ancient capital of the Persian empire. The Persian Achaemenid shah, Darius the Great (r. 522–486 BCE), built Persepolis and it served as the symbolic seat of Persian kingship even after later dynasties had built new capitals. The Sassanids followed Zoroastrianism and, in 954, when 'Adud al-Dawla visited the Palace of Darius at Persepolis, he brought a Zoroastrian priest to read him the Persian inscriptions there.

Visiting Persepolis and enacting Sassanid rituals there allowed 'Adud al-Dawla to build his legitimacy by embodying older, more established forms of royal authority. In the past, this visit has been interpreted as merely Buyid "interest in their Iranian roots."[46] But it was more than this: the Buyids, and especially 'Adud al-Dawla, wanted to establish their legitimacy by embodying older, more established forms of royal authority. The Buyids did not have a prestigious royal heritage. As Clifford Geertz has argued in "Centres, Kings, and Charisma: Reflections on the Symbolics of Power," in a society where kingship was considered sacred, there was a special, sacral quality to bodily taking the place of a previous sovereign (122). Visiting Persepolis and enacting the rituals of previous Persian kings would have made 'Adud al-Dawla look more legitimate. Aziz al-Azmeh, in *Muslim Kingship*, argued that this tactic, of visiting the palace of a past king, was common in the medieval world to appropriate the power attributed to a past authority (12–13). By physically embodying the royal role of the previous ruler, the worldly and political power of that king was mystically transferred into the new ruler (31). In order for 'Adud al-Dawla to compete successfully with the power of the 'Abbasid caliph (and with other local leaders), he had to adopt another, competing form of royal authority, such as Sassanid kingship.

In other words: kings are made, not born, they crafted royal authority via elaborate rituals and ceremonies. Thus, when 'Adud al-Dawla visited Persepolis, had the Persian inscriptions there read to him by a Zoroastrian priest, and left his own inscriptions there, he claimed Sassanid authority and legitimacy. Visiting the palaces and monuments associated with ancient Persian kings allowed him to acquire the royal glory of those kings. The Persians called royal glory *farr,* and they defined it as a special quality possessed by their kings. It originally meant life force or splendour and, over time, came to mean victory and fortune. *Farr* was the symbolic source of legitimacy for Iranian rulers, believed to originate from the Zoroastrian god Ahura Mazda and then transferred over time from the god to the Sassanids. This divine lineage gave the Sassanid king omnipotent powers and absolute authority over the world. 'Adud al-Dawla tapped into that history to serve the Buyids.

'Adud al-Dawla, however, also made a significant change to the ancient Persian *farr*. When he visited Persepolis, he left his own inscriptions at Persepolis in Arabic, not in Persian. Seeing as the ancient Persians looked down on the Arabs, calling them uncivilized lizard-eaters, this choice was not accidental. Instead, it revealed how 'Adud al-Dawla tried to bring together Arab and Persian forms of identity. 'Adud al-Dawla had been educated in Arabic. But he was among the first generation of Buyid leaders to speak Arabic—his father and two uncles did not. Leaving this Arabic inscription at Persepolis, where the commemoration of military victories had been common in ancient times, suggests a deliberate choice about how 'Adud al-Dawla wanted to portray his own authority in a rapidly changing Islamic society. Furthermore, 'Adud al-Dawla brought Zoroastrian priests to Persepolis with him, to read aloud the inscriptions there, both the ones from previous kings and his own. In his own inscriptions, he celebrated his recent military victories. These were key aspects of the ritual: in addition to divine favour, the Sassanid shahs needed victory in battle along with acclamation of the Zoroastrian priesthood and the nobility to confirm their royal status.

With these inscriptions, 'Adud al-Dawla stressed the continuity of his rule not only with the Sassanid dynasty, but also with the 'Abbasid caliphs, who also modelled their symbolic claims to kingship on Sassanid rituals. While the 'Abbasids grounded their claims to authority in Islamic doctrines, they also adopted aspects of Sassanid rituals to articulate their own legitimacy. For example, the language and ritual of the oaths that the caliphs took when they took power echoed the oaths of Sassanid kings.[47] Furthermore, as discussed in the previous chapter, Baghdad had been designed to imitate Sassanid palace cities.

By visiting Persepolis and having a Zoroastrian priest read aloud the inscribed exploits of former pre-Islamic Iranian shahs, and then by leaving an Arabic inscription detailing his own victories, 'Adud al-Dawla affirmed his own place in the continuum of historical rule between the pre-Islamic and the Islamic. He brought these two traditions together by emphasizing his Sassanid roots in a form that made them both Arabic and Islamic. Framing his Sassanid roots in terms of both Arab ethnic identity and Muslim identity allowed 'Adud al-Dawla to use the past to create a viable form of Buyid kingship for the present in a way that directly competed with the legitimacy of the 'Abbasid caliphs (and the Fatimids).

Ideal Muslim Rulers

'Adud al-Dawla and the Buyids did not only claim to be descendants of Persian kingship. They also buttressed their legitimacy by claiming the Islamic past in ways that emphasized that they were better rulers than the 'Abbasids. For example, in addition to using the title *Shahanshah*, 'Adud al-Dawla also adopted the title "The Just Prince" (*al-Amir al-'Adil*). In the tenth century, the title "The Just Prince" would have most clearly reminded audiences of the second caliph, 'Umar b. al-Khattab (d. 644), who, according to Tayeb El-Hirbi in *Parable and Politics in Early Islamic History*, was often called "the Just Ruler" (*al-Sultan al-'Adil*) and portrayed as the quintessential Arab in historical chronicles and credited with the conquest of Iran (77–89).

Shi'is often had a negative view of the Caliph 'Umar because of his opposition to 'Ali b. Abi Talib. However, claiming the authority of 'Umar allowed 'Adud al-Dawla to accomplish two significant rhetorical goals: first, he could embody the memory of the Muslim leader who was often depicted in the chronicles as the quintessential Arab or Bedouin; second, he could link himself with the Caliph 'Umar's reputation as a great political leader and the founder of many of the institutions of the first Islamic state.

Likening himself to Caliph 'Umar allowed 'Adud al-Dawla to buttress his claims to Arabness. El-Hibri's work has extensively explored how the first four caliphs were remembered in Arabic chronicles and, as he argued, ninth-century historical works emphasized the Arabism of the second caliph and his victory over the Persian Sassanid Empire. Muslim historians stressed 'Umar's conquest of the Persians through the frequent use of "Arab imagery and literary expressions in [...] descriptions of Muslim battles on the Persian front," which depicted 'Umar as the founder of the Arab-Islamic state and its champion over Persian forces (84). These chronicles emphasized the Arab pedigree of the caliph 'Umar by idealizing his relationship with the Bedouin and by relating stories of his asceticism that feature his disapproval of the general richness of Persian luxuries. The motivation for these portrayals lay in a desire to romanticize the Arab ancestry of the 'Abbasid caliphs during an era of increasing Persian influence.

In the eighth and ninth-century chronicles, 'Umar was best known for his skills as an administrator and as the founder of many of the institutions of Islamic rule. Borrowing 'Umar's legacy helped 'Adud al-Dawla argue that he was re-establishing the stability and greatness of 'Abbasid Baghdad, which had descended into famine and civil war. The reign of al-Muqtadir (r. 908–932), the 'Abbasid caliph who was appointed as a minor and was generally considered to be controlled by his advisors, has been characterized as the 'Abbasid caliphate at its weakest. The period featured tremendous territorial losses, corruption, and sectarian rebellions. Al-Muqtadir was actually dethroned twice before finally being assassinated.

To contrast himself with the inadequacy of 'Abbasid rule in Baghdad, 'Adud al-Dawla sponsored histories that emphasized his own ability to re-establish order in the city. For example, Miskawayh's *The Experience of Nations (Tajarab al-'Umam)* related that, under the Caliph Muqtadir, rioting broke out in Baghdad after the price of bread rose precipitously. Mobs plundered shops and then assembled at the gate of the caliphal palace. The people attacked the public mosques of Baghdad, breaking the pulpits and interrupting public worship. Their rioting did not stop until al-Muqtadir ordered the shops and storehouses that belonged to high-ranking members of the court to be opened to sell wheat and barley at a reduced price. In 940 and 941, just before the Buyids conquered the city, Miskawayh again reported rioting in Baghdad when prices rose and poor maintenance led local canals to burst their banks. The prices for foodstuffs in Baghdad were so high that, according to Miskawayh, "the people ate grass and there were numerous deaths; so many that several people were buried in one grave without washing or prayer." Mobs attacked the homes of the wealthy and the city devolved into civil war, with factions attacking infrastructure, such as bridges and the prison. The violence was so great that the caliph, his family, and many of the leading citizens abandoned the city.

Miskawayh's history covered from the Prophet Muhammad to the reign of 'Adud al-Dawla. Miskawayh served as a bureaucrat and, as such, had great respect for those bureaucrats who effectively ran an administration. His history emphasized the good management of state affairs when he witnessed it and harshly judged poor administrations led by greedy and corrupt bureaucrats. His praise of good administration, however, was never aimed at the tenth-century 'Abbasids; he emphasized how the 'Abbasid caliphs were, at best, uninvolved and, at worst, drunkards. He even included an anecdote about one caliph being too drunk to attend to his duties.

Instead, Miskawayh helped the Buyids claim authority by emphasizing 'Adud al-Dawla's competence as an administrator in contrast with the ruin caused by the 'Abbasid caliphs. For example, when 'Adud al-Dawla took over Baghdad, the caliph's palace was in ruins. 'Adud al-Dawla ordered the repair and renovation of the palace, filling it with new furnishings and hiring more servants. 'Adud al-Dawla paid for all of this himself, giving the caliph money, clothing, furniture, horses, slaves, and instruments. He also reconfirmed the caliph's possession of "the estates of the service," which had been withdrawn under previous Buyid rulers.

Miskawayh buttressed Buyid legitimacy by using existing standards of an ideal Muslim ruler to describe 'Adud al-Dawla. The idea of the ideal Muslim ruler transcended sectarian categories and had roots in pre-Islamic Persian history. An eighth-century courtier who served the 'Abbasids, Ibn al-Muqaffa' (d. 756), wrote the earliest surviving work on ideal kingship, stressing that the ideal Muslim king maintained stability, paid the army a regular salary, remained informed of developments in his territory, and established religious orthodoxy. He was God-fearing, competent in politics and administration, and closely supervised his appointed officials to guard against corruption. Later Muslim authors, such as al-Jahiz (d. 868) and al-Mawardi (d. 1058), emphasized similar qualities.

Miskawayh emphasized 'Adud al-Dawla's fulfilment of the qualities of an ideal Muslim ruler and implied that 'Adud al-Dawla was a *more* legitimate ruler than the 'Abbasid caliph, who had let Baghdad fall into chaos. Miskawayh argued that 'Adud al-Dawla preserved the security of Baghdad, protected the people, defeated his enemies, made the lands more productive, and restored the empire to its glory, saving Iraq from a period of chaos and corruption that began during the reign of the 'Abbasids. Miskawayh described how 'Adud al-Dawla restored order and grandeur to the 'Abbasid capital of Baghdad, which had long been the capital of the Islamic world:

> 'Adud al-Dawla ordered the houses and streets of Baghdad to be rebuilt, as they had been injured partly by arson, partly by demolition. They were a mere heap. He began with the public mosques, which were in an absolutely ruinous condition, spending a vast sum on them. Such of the buildings as were beyond repair were demolished by his order and replaced with solid erections, which were raised high, furnished, and decorated. He ordered the remunerations of the managers, muezzins, prayer-leaders, and readers to be regularly paid, and allowances to be provided for the strangers and poor who took refuge in them; all this had been neglected and unthought-of. Next he ordered the res-

toration of such suburban mosques as were out of repair,
and restored their trust-funds (5:443–44).

'Adud al-Dawla's building program and periodic works restored
Baghdad to its previous glory, thereby demonstrating that
he was more qualified than both his Buyid predecessors and
the 'Abbasid caliphs to lead the Islamic world. These claims
to legitimacy and authority were made without reference to
sectarian concerns.

Reactions to the Buyids

Sunni reactions to the Buyids were more complex than a simple binary of Sunni versus Shi'i. Overall, the tenth-century
Sunni sources depicted Shi'i Buyid rule as a reprieve from
the chaos and civil war that had plagued Baghdad. These
sources did not portray opposition to the takeover of the Buyids in terms of Sunni opposition to Shi'i rule. While the Buyids
were a Shi'i dynasty, the Buyid amirate was predominately a
military-administrative position concerned with re-establishing enough stability over 'Abbasid territories to collect tax
revenues and minimize external threats. The Buyids did not
attempt to control or police the religious activities of the Muslims of Baghdad.

Local tenth-century Sunni depictions of the Buyids do not
even express opposition to Buyid rule. Two tenth-century
Sunni accounts of life under the Buyids survive, written by
Sunnis living in Baghdad. It is striking that neither of these
two tenth-century Sunni authors living under Shi'i Buyid rule
conveyed any distress about living under and working for a
Shi'i administration. Instead, they were predominately concerned with popular religious movements led by Sufis, Islamic
mystics, and the general decline of Baghdad as the capital of
the Muslim world. Neither of these contemporary Sunni wit-
nesses to Shi'i Buyid rule mentioned the Shi'i identity of the
Buyid amirs nor the public practice of Shi'i religious rituals.

Hilal ibn al-Muhassin al-Sabi (d. 1056), who wrote a history
of the rules and protocols of the 'Abbasid court, emphasized

how the Shi'i Buyids and their administrators treated the Sunni 'Abbasid caliph with respect. Al-Sabi (969–1056) was born a Sabian, a member of a Christian sect, but converted to Islam. He served a Buyid *vizier* early in his career and wrote a treatise on the rules and protocols of the 'Abbasid court, *Traditions of the Caliphal Court* (*Rusum Dar al-Khalifa*). While Hilal al-Sabi did not openly declare his sectarian identity, his writings commanded a tremendous degree of respect for the 'Abbasid caliph and the opening of his treatise suggests a Sunni identity. He opened his work with a prayer for the consolidation of the caliphate, referred to the 'Abbasid caliph as "the best and most illustrious," "the unrivalled imam," and "the great and undisputed vicegerent of Allah," and asserted that "the caliphate derives from the prophethood; it enjoys thereby the highest and noblest degree of dignity and excellence." He also related a story of how a powerful Buyid administrator, al-Muhallabi (d. 963), who served as the *vizier* of the first Buyid amir in Baghdad, once dared raise his voice in the presence of the Sunni 'Abbasid caliph. The caliph, incensed at his lack of respect, evicted al-Muhallabi from court until he had apologized and begged to be readmitted, saying. "I am a servant; I neither intended to misbehave nor to offend; but as my voice is loud, my speech is loud too. When I am dismissed in this manner [from your court], my prestige will decline, my influence will cease, and my friends will desert me."[48] In this anecdote, Hilal al-Sabi did not mention the Shi'i identity of the Buyids but used the story to show how the Sunni caliph still possessed sacred authority that was respected by the Buyids and their bureaucrats. Overall, Hilal al-Sabi emphasized that the Shi'i Buyid amirs treated the Sunni 'Abbasid caliphs with tremendous respect and, in turn, received extensive privileges and robes of honour symbolic of the sacred authority of the caliph.[49]

Al-Tanukhi (d. 994) was a Sunni religious scholar who began his career in the bureaucracy of the Buyid amirs as a religious judge in Iraq and Iran, then later held various positions in the Buyid administration in Baghdad. He wrote a history of tenth-century Baghdad society, entitled *Conversations and Recollections* (*Nishwar al-muhadarah wa akhbar al-mud-hakarah*), while living in Baghdad and serving in the Buyid administration. Al-Tanukhi, a Sunni religious scholar, also did not comment on the Shiʻi identity of the Buyids. Rather, he focused on a broad deterioration of religious knowledge among Sunni religious scholars and the growing popularity of Sufi movements. He blamed both of these problems on the "lowering of the caliphate," which he blamed on the Sunni ʻAbbasids, whom he accused of selling religious offices and appointing unqualified candidates to religious offices, leading to disrespect for Sunni religious officials.

According to al-Tanukhi, corrupt, ignorant religious officials were more common than honest, educated ones. He lamented, "the times are wrong, and our profession is spoiled."[50] Further, al-Tanukhi criticized the rise of popular religious movements in Baghdad. He did not identify these movements as Sunni or Shiʻi, but characterized them as led by Sufi *shaykhs*, whom al-Tanukhi accused of deceiving the people with tricks. During the tenth century, Sufis were not yet considered orthodox or acceptable by Sunni religious scholars and al-Tanukhi filled his account of life in Baghdad with stories of popular religious figures which he considered to be tricksters or heretics. In one story, al-Tanukhi railed against a Sufi who claimed he had control over the material world. To prove this, the Sufi would offer to plunge his hand into boiling oil without experiencing pain.[51]

Neither Hilal al-Sabi or al-Tanukhi mentioned local strife in Baghdad caused by sectarian conflict or by the Shiʻi orientation of the Buyid amirs. For these two tenth-century Sunni authors living under Shiʻi Buyid rule, the most significant issue facing contemporary Baghdad was the overall deterioration of the city due to the weakening power of the Sunni ʻAbbasid caliphs. This decline had not been caused by the Shiʻi Buyids, nor did the Buyids destroy the sacred power of the Sunni ʻAbbasid caliphs. Neither Hilal al-Sabi nor al-Tanukhi saw local concerns through a lens of sectarian conflict and neither author described the Shiʻi Buyids in terms of their Shiʻi identity.

Notes

[41] Joel L. Kraemer, *Humanism in the Renaissance of Islam: The Cultural Revival During the Buyid Age* (Leiden: Brill, 1992), 53–54.

[42] The first generation consisted of three brothers: 'Imad al-Dawla, Rukn al-Dawla, and Mu'izz al-Dawla. 'Imad al-Dawla was the eldest brother and the senior member of the triumvirate. 'Adud al-Dawla was the son of Rukn al-Dawla, the governor of Rayy, but his uncle 'Imad al-Dawla, who died without sons, appointed him as his successor in Fars.

[43] Abu Ishaq Ibrahim b. Hilal al-Sabi, *Muntaza' min Kitab al-Taji fi akhbar al-Dawla al-Daylamiya*, in *Arabic Texts Concerning the History of the Zaydi Imams of Tabaristan, Daylaman, and Gilan*, ed. Wilferd Madelung (Beirut: Ergon, 1987), 12–13. All translations from al-Sabi's *Kitab al-Taji* are my own.

[44] Mutanabbi has been translated by several scholars. For the translation here, see Arthur Wormhoudt, *The Diwan of Abu Tayyib Ahmad ibn al-Husayn al-Mutanabbi* (Chicago: ABC International Group, 2002), 511.

[45] Here, I preferred Margaret Larkin's translation: Larkin, *Al-Mutanabbi: Voice of the 'Abbasid Poetic Ideal* (Oxford: Oneworld, 2008), 87.

[46] John J. Donohue made this comment in "Three Buwayhid Inscriptions," *Arabica* 20, no. 1 (February 1973), 74–80, where he also published images and text of the Buyid inscriptions at Persepolis.

[47] For a discussion of how 'Abbasid rituals followed Sassanid precedents, see Andrew Marsham, *Rituals of Islamic Monarchy: Accession and Succession in the First Muslim Empire* (Edinburgh: Edinburgh University Press, 2009), 208–9.

[48] Hilal al-Sabi, *Rusum Dar al-Khalifah*, Mikha'il 'Awwad, ed. (Baghdad: al-'Ani Press, 1964), 42–43. Here, I have used the translation from Hilal al-Sabi, *The Rules and Regulations of the Abbasid Court*, trans. Ellie Salem (Beirut: The American University of Beirut Press, 1977), 31.

[49] Al-Sabi, *Rusum*, 128–31.

[50] Abu 'Ali al-Muhassin b. 'Ali al-Tanukhi, *Nishwar al-muhadarah wa akhbar al-mudhakarah*, Abboud al-Shalji (Bayrut: Matabi' Dar Sadir, 1971). "Nishwar al-Muhadarah" literally means something like "chewing the cud of conversation." Tanukhi's *Nishwar al-Muhadarah* has been translated by D.S. Margoliouth as *The Table-talk of a Mesopotamian Judge* (London: Royal Asiatic Society, 1922). I will cite Tanukhi's Arabic as well as Margoliouth's translations. Tanukhi, *Nishwar*, 118 and Margoliouth, 128.

[51] Tanukhi, *Nishwar*, 81, 85, and 171–72. Margoliouth, 87 and 92.

Conclusion:
Reactions to the Shi'i Century

To a large extent, we have been discussing something that historians call historical memory, which refers to how groups or societies remember past events and how that memory can change over time. Historical memory includes how we remember the past as well as how we interpret representations of the past. Mainly, it means that we need to remember that histories are written within specific contexts and often serve specific purposes. Even if past historians aimed to be objective, they had their own biases that informed their writing. Thus, rather than viewing history as some kind of truth that we can discover about the past, historians more often view historical sources as a lens through which we can interpret how past peoples saw themselves and their world. Historical memory is not fiction, but it has been constructed by a society, usually to emphasize something that the society values.

These kinds of analyses have been done on other periods in Islamic history, but not for the Fatimids and Buyids. For example, Jacob Lassner, in *Islamic Revolution and Historical Memory*, analysed how the 'Abbasids wrote early Islamic history after they overthrew the 'Umayyads. He demonstrated how these histories were not intended to preserve the truth of past events but, rather, to argue that the 'Umayyads were illegitimate and the 'Abbasids represented a return to the tradition of the Prophet. Scholars of historical memory, such as Patrick Geary in *Phantoms of Remembrance*, argue that reconstructing historical memory allows us to understand what was important to the people who constructed it in the first place. Much of this book has focused on Fatimid and Buyid historical memory: how did they want to be remembered? How did they link themselves with the past in ways that made them seem legitimate to the people they ruled? Were those claims inherently sectarian?

During the eleventh and twelfth centuries, the political fortunes of the Middle East changed dramatically. This period saw the influx of new groups of Turkic peoples who took over political control of the region. In 1055, the Seljuks, a Turkic dynasty, conquered Baghdad and ousted the Buyids. The Fatimids lasted more than another century; they lost power in 1171 when one of their *viziers*, Salah al-Din al-Ayyubi (often better known as Saladin), ousted a weak Fatimid caliph and declared himself the ruler of Fatimid territory, establishing the rule of the Ayyubid dynasty.

Both the Seljuks and the Ayyubids arose out of the influx of Turkic peoples into the Middle East and made their Sunni identity a significant part of their claims to legitimacy. The Seljuks claimed to be saving the 'Abbasid caliph from the Shi'ism of the Buyids while Saladin immediately declared that he was ruling Egypt in the name of the Sunni 'Abbasid caliph. Because these two dynasties foregrounded their Sunni identity in their efforts to articulate their legitimacy and authority to rule, historians often called this era the Sunni Revival.

Historians of the medieval Islamic world have long recognized how both Sunnis and Shi'is used early Islamic history to create narratives of legitimacy. And they have also recognized how the Sunni revival reveals a sustained effort to legitimize new non-Arab rulers in the region. The construction of the Shi'i century as a narrative of sectarian conflict is significant because it persists and affects how modern scholars view early and medieval Islamic history. As discussed in Chapter One, we tend to view Sunni Islam as original and normative while reducing all other forms of Islam to heterodoxy. Further, we often presume a primordial hostility between

Sunnis and Shi'is that diminishes the complexity of medieval Muslim identity.

For example, an early twentieth-century work on Buyid history explained that:

> The Mahdite Shi'ahs, the Karmathians and the Fatimids [...] continued the Kharijite struggle against the Caliphate, an indication that the old Islamic regime was at an end. The revival of the essentially old oriental ideas in Shi'ism at the expense of Islam constitutes the distinguishing feature of the spiritual movements of the 4th/10th century.[52]

This analysis classifies all Shi'i millenarian movements, the *Qarmatiyya,* who were an offshoot of the Isma'ilis; the Fatimid Isma'ilis; and the *Kharijis,* who formed a diverse movement in their own right and were generally anti-Shi'i, as essentially the same. It reduces a diverse range of tenth-century Muslim movements to a single characteristic: not Sunni. Further, it implies that all of these non-Sunni movements could be considered anti-Islamic because they were mixing pre-Islamic "old oriental ideas" with Islam.

Although the above example dates to the 1930s, analyses that further the sectarian narrative of the tenth century are still common. Here, an article written on the early Ghaznavids (963–1186) for the *Cambridge History of Iran* in the mid-1970s reduces the complex political history of the late tenth and early eleventh centuries to simple sectarian conflict:

> It would not have been difficult for the sultan [Mahmud of Ghazna] to find a plausible pretext for meddling in Buyid affairs: [...] the Buyids were Shi'is, and as long as they held Baghdad, the 'Abbasid caliph could not be considered a free agent.[53]

The Sunni ruler Mahmud of Ghazna (d. 1030) certainly rationalized his invasion of Buyid territory in the name of 'saving' the 'Abbasid caliph from the Shi'i Buyids, but the above description oversimplifies the actual political situation in Baghdad and the concerns of Mahmud of Ghazna. First, there had been many periods where the 'Abbasid caliph could not be considered a free agent. Second, although the Buyid amirs served as political rulers in Iraq and Iran, as Eric Hanne argues in *Putting the Caliph in His Place*, that does not mean that the 'Abbasid caliphs were powerless. Mahmud of Ghazna may have found it useful to depict himself as the defender of Sunni orthodoxy, but his motivations were not nearly so simplistic and cannot necessarily be taken at face value.

More recent examples of this tendency to see the tenth century only through the lens of a narrative of sectarian conflict are harder to identify because the study of the dynasties of the Shi'i Century has become relatively marginalized in modern scholarship on the medieval Middle East. There is a lively community of scholars who study the Fatimids, but there has been relatively little research on the Buyids in the past thirty years. These two groups also tend to be studied in isolation, as Shi'i anomalies not necessarily linked with the larger processes of Islamic history. There are almost no studies that analyse the broader tenth century and the ways that the Fatimids and Buyids, together and via their competition, defined Shi'i identity.

Historians have emphasized the sectarian identity and the binary between Sunnis and Shi'is because this was how later medieval Muslim sources, written after the fall of the Fatimids and Buyids, remembered this era. In order to illustrate the broad changing depictions of sectarian identity from the tenth to the eleventh century, we can compare two writers who lived approximately a century apart: al-Muqaddasi (d. ca. 1000) and Nizam al-Mulk (d. 1092). Al-Muqaddasi was a scholar from Jerusalem who travelled the Middle East between the years of 965–985, during the zenith of Fatimid and Buyid rule. He wrote *The Best Divisions for Knowledge of the Regions* (*Ahsan al-Taqasim fi Ma'rifat al-Aqalim*) to provide a resource for "devout and upright people" who might draw upon the story of his travels for entertainment or profit (1–2).[54] Nizam al-Mulk served as the *vizier* to the Seljuks in the period immediately following the fall of the Buyids in Iraq and Iran. He wrote a famous guide to future political leaders, called *The Book of Government* (*Siyasat-nama*), and founded a series of colleges dedicated to teaching Sunni religious law that were remembered, in his name, as the *Nizamiyya*.

The difference in the way that these two men, one from the tenth century and the other the eleventh, saw sectarian identity is striking and reveals how attitudes about sectarianism had shifted in those hundred years of Shi'i rule. Al-Muqaddasi marvelled at the variety of religions found within the cities he visited, painting a picture of a tenth-century Islamic world filled with diverse Muslim identities. In his travels, he named many types of Muslims. He discussed non-Sunni groups, such as Shi'is and *Kharijis*, but also philosophical movements that transcended sect, such as the *Murji'a* and *Mu'tazilis*, and schools of Sunni religious law. He also identified Muslims who followed different types of religious authorities and Muslims who read the Qur'an in different ways (37–43). In Baghdad, he described the city's population of Zoroastrians, Christians, and Jews. He noted that Baghdad's Muslims were mostly Sunnis who followed the Hanbali school of religious law, but mentioned that there were several kinds of Muslims living there. In Fatimid Cairo, he identified both Sunnis and Shi'is, stressing that they lived together and intermingled. He did not mention sectarian strife between Sunnis and Shi'is in either Fatimid Cairo or Buyid Baghdad.

Al-Muqaddasi did criticize Muslim religious practices that he disagreed with; he was not merely an aloof narrator. But he mainly reserved his disapproval for the religious practices of rural Muslims, whom he found to be ill-informed and, at times, heretical. He did not describe these practices in any detail, but singled out the non-urban Muslims of Arabia and Yemen as "fanatical heretics" (82). As an educated, urban Muslim, however, al-Muqaddasi's distaste for non-urban religious practices was not surprising.

In his critiques of certain types of Muslim practice, however, al-Muqaddasi did not single out Shi'i practices as heterodox or problematic. He was interested in these differences and explained them to his audience (which perhaps also suggests that broad knowledge of the differences was not widespread outside of circles of religious scholars). He noted that differences in practice existed, but did not offer judgment on these differences. The differences that he mentioned were that Shi'is allowed temporary marriage (*mut'a*), triple repudiation for divorce, had slightly different rules about purification for prayer, and used a slightly different phrase in their call to prayer (theirs included the refrain, "come to the best of works"). He did not mention any conflicts caused by these differences (40).

Al-Muqaddasi visited both Buyid Baghdad and Fatimid Cairo; his main interests there were political and economic. He lamented the disintegrating fortunes of Baghdad:

> Every heart yearns for [Baghdad]; every battle is fought over it, and every hand is raised to defend it. It is too renowned to need description, more glorious than we could possibly portray it, and is indeed beyond praise [...]. However, the authority of the *khalifs* [caliphs] declined, the city deteriorated, and the population dwindled. The City of Peace is now desolate: the Mosque alone is frequented on Fridays, and otherwise the whole place is deserted (100).

He discussed how Baghdad was the seat of the 'Abbasid caliphs and noted their decline, but he did not mention the Buyid amirs directly. Instead, he commented on how the Daylamites, the Buyids' kingroup, now controlled Baghdad and had ended the political power of the caliphs (110). Al-Muqaddasi did not mention that the Daylamites were Shi'i, that there had been sectarian conflict in the city, or that there were public Shi'i rituals observed there.

In comparison, al-Muqaddasi celebrated the development of Fustat/Cairo under the Fatimids:

> Fustat [Cairo] is a metropolis in every sense of the word; here are together all the departments of government administration, and moreover, it is the seat of the Commander of the Faithful [...]. Its name is renowned, its glory increased; for truly it is the capital city of Egypt. It has superseded Baghdad, and is the glory of Islam, and is the marketplace for all mankind. It is more sublime than the City of Peace [Baghdad]. It is the storehouse of the Occident, the entrepot

of the Orient, and is crowded with people at the time of the Pilgrimage festival. Among the capitals there is none more populous than it, and it abounds in noble and learned men. Its goods of commerce and specialties are remarkable, its markets splendid and handsome. Nowhere in the realm of Islam is there a mosque more crowded than here, nor people more handsomely adorned, no shore with a greater number of boats (166).

Al-Muqaddasi never mentioned the Fatimids by name in his discussion of Cairo, nor did he mention that the rulers were Shi'i. Instead, he focused on the economic development of Cairo: the city had a rich, active market based on trade with both Europe and the Middle East. He discussed how the mosques were crowded and the city was an important stop on the annual pilgrimage to Mecca. He did not mention anything related to sectarianism or Shi'ism in his discussion of Cairo.

Nizam al-Mulk, writing approximately a century later, had a strikingly different view of non-Sunni Muslims. In *The Book of Government*, this was how he explained Shi'ism:

> Whenever the Batinis [Shi'is] have appeared they have had a name or a nickname, and in every city and province they have been known by a different title; but in essence they are all the same. In Aleppo and Egypt they call them Isma'ilis; in Qum, Kashan, Tabaristan and Sabzvar they are called Shi'ites; in Baghdad, Transoxiana, and Ghaznain they are known as Qarmatis, in Kufa as Mubarakis, in Basra as Rawandis and Burqa'is, in Rayy as Khalafis, in Gurgan as The Wearers of Red, in Syria as The Wearers of White, in the West as Sa'idis, in al-Ahsa and Bahrain as Jannabis, and in Isfahan as Batinis; whereas they call themselves The Didactics and other such names. But their whole purpose is only to abolish Islam and to lead mankind astray (238).[55]

While al-Muqaddasi seemed fascinated by the diversity of medieval Muslim identities, Nizam al-Mulk reduced that diversity to a binary of Sunni versus Shi'i. He identified all non-Sunni movements as *batini*s who sought to "abolish Islam and lead mankind astray." It had been less than a generation since the fall of the Buyids, and the Fatimids still ruled in

Cairo, but it was already possible to see the process by which the history of Muslim sectarianism was being rewritten *ex post facto* as a sectarian narrative. Instead of al-Muqaddasi's easy description of Fatimid and Buyid rule and the diversity of medieval Muslim identities, we find later scholars following Nizam al-Mulk's model, depicting non-Sunni movements as trying to "abolish Islam and to lead mankind astray." By the eleventh and twelfth centuries, Muslim scholars and chroniclers focused nearly exclusively on the Shi'i orientation of the Fatimids and Buyids, depicting it as a source of chaos and strife in the Muslim community.

Shifting Portrayals of the Shi'i Century

While a comprehensive survey of later sources is not possible in such a short volume, in this conclusion I want to present a few examples of how sources from after the twelfth century portrayed the Fatimids and Buyids. These portrayals were often strikingly different from the ways that tenth-century sources, even those written by Sunni religious scholars, discussed the sectarian identity of the Fatimids and Buyids.

Later sources on the Fatimids tended to portray the Fatimids as violent persecutors of Sunnis who cursed the first three caliphs (the *Rashidun*) and betrayed even the most basic norms of Islamic society. For example, Ibn 'Idhari (d. after 1313) lived in North Africa in the late thirteenth and early fourteenth centuries. Detailed biographical information on Ibn 'Idhari did not survive, so we do not know his sectarian background. He wrote a history of North Africa and Spain entitled *The Report on North Africa* (*al-Bayan al-Mughrib*). In his history, he portrayed the Shi'i Fatimids in clear terms of sectarian conflict: he claimed that the Shi'i Fatimids publicly cursed the first three caliphs and violently persecuted local Sunnis. He also claimed that the Fatimids did not follow even basic ideas acceptable to Muslims, saying that they cursed the Prophet Muhammad and his family, abandoned religious law, and had sexual relations with women who were forbidden to them, such as their own daughters (I: 216). None of the tenth-century sources mentioned these kinds of practices and it is difficult to imagine that tenth-century Sunni religious scholars would not have mentioned the Fatimid caliphs cursing the Prophet and his family (among the other accusations made against them).

We can also see a difference in coverage in the way that our sources discuss competition among Sunni groups. For example, as discussed in Chapter Three, relations between the Fatimids and Sunni religious scholars were often fraught. In 909, a Fatimid governor executed two Sunni Maliki scholars in Qayrawan. In tenth-century sources written by Sunni religious scholars living in Qayrawan, they blamed the execution on competition between the Hanafis and Malikis. They also dated the execution to the period before the first Fatimid caliph, al-Mahdi, had reached Qayrawan (when the town was being ruled by one of his governors). Later sources, dating from after the Fatimids lost control of North Africa, however, related this event in a strikingly different manner. Abu Bakr al-Maliki (d. 1148), a Sunni Maliki scholar living in Qayrawan, made this event about Fatimid persecution of Sunnis and changed the timeline of events to blame al-Mahdi specifically. Al-Maliki related that al-Mahdi himself summoned the two Maliki scholars to his presence and commanded them to testify that the Fatimid caliph (al-Mahdi) was the Messenger of God. When they refused, al-Maliki's twelfth-century account claimed that al-Mahdi directly ordered their execution.[56] The tenth-century sources portray this incident as part of inter-Sunni competition while al-Maliki places the story within a broader narrative of sectarian conflict, depicting the Sunni Malikis as martyred for refusing to compromise their beliefs in the face of Shi'i Fatimid oppression.

Later sources on the Buyids emphasize the Shi'i identity of the Buyids as the defining characteristic of their rule, giving the impression that Buyid policy decisions were greatly informed by the rulers' Shi'i orientation, that the Sunni 'Abbasid caliph was held hostage and disrespected by the Buyids, and that sectarian violence was rampant in Baghdad. As you will remember from Chapter Four, these portrayals strikingly conflict with the tenth-century portrayals of Buyid rule in Baghdad, which mostly ignored their Shi'i identity and emphasized how the Buyids had ended a period of chaos in the city.

For example, Ibn al-Jawzi (d. 1201), a Hanbali Sunni religious scholar, wrote a comprehensive historical chronicle in the twelfth century that modern historians often cite for the history of Baghdad: *al-Muntazam fi ta'rikh al-muluk wa al-umam*. In his history, Ibn al-Jawzi frequently claimed that there was rampant sectarian violence in tenth-century Baghdad. He reported that Sunni–Shi'i riots occurred in the years 949, 951, 959, 960, 962, and 964. He also claimed that the Shi'is of Baghdad vandalized Sunni mosques in the city.[57] Significantly, none of the tenth-century sources mentioned these issues (neither the Sunni sources nor sources sponsored by the Buyids themselves). Some of the tenth-century Buyid-sponsored sources mentioned civil unrest in Baghdad, but they identified the source of the conflict as power clashes between the military, the Buyid amirs, and other local challengers for power, conflicts which did not fall along Sunni–Shi'i lines. Neither of the tenth-century Sunni accounts mentioned sectarian violence in Shi'i Buyid controlled Baghdad.

Several later sources also claimed that the Buyids sponsored public Shi'i rituals in Baghdad, which led to sectarian violence: Ibn al-Jawzi, mentioned above, Ibn al-Athir (d. 1233), and Ibn Kathir (d. 1373). All three sources related that the first Buyid amir in Baghdad ordered public commemorations of Shi'i religious holidays in 963 and 964. According to the thirteenth and fourteenth-century Sunni sources, the public practice of these new Shi'i rituals so incensed Baghdad's Sunni community that they instituted counter-rituals in protest.[58] The counter-rituals mentioned by the later sources would have been particularly antagonistic toward Shi'is but, strikingly, none of the tenth-century sources mention them—not the contemporary Sunni sources nor the Buyid-sponsored sources.

Neither public celebrations of Shi'i rituals nor Sunni counter-celebrations appear in the tenth-century histories of Buyid rule. Although it could be argued that tenth-century sources might avoid mentioning sectarian rioting, there would be no reason for Buyid-sponsored sources to avoid mentioning religious rituals sponsored by the Buyids. Buyid-sponsored religious rituals would have been one way that the Buyids claimed legitimacy. There may very well have been public Shi'i rituals in Baghdad during the tenth century, but their absence from the tenth-century sources suggests that these rituals were probably small, not sponsored by the Shi'i Buyid state, and not as significant as portrayed by the Sunni sources written after the fall of the Buyid dynasty.

The post tenth-century Sunni sources also portray the Shi'i identity of the Buyids as the primary motivation for all government decisions. For example, Mu'izz al-Dawla (d. 967), the first Buyid amir in Baghdad, deposed the Sunni 'Abbasid caliph al-Mustakfi (d. 949) eleven days after conquering Baghdad. The twelfth-century Sunni chronicler Ibn al-Athir used the deposition as evidence that the Buyids pursued a Shi'i religious agenda. Ibn al-Athir claimed that Mu'izz al-Dawla had wanted to appoint a descendant of 'Ali to the caliphate but was warned by advisors that an 'Alid caliph would have the power to challenge Buyid authority on religious grounds.[59] According to Ibn al-Jawzi's twelfth-century account, Mu'izz al-Dawla considered two 'Alid candidates: Abu al-Hasan (d. 936), a Zaydi Imam in Yemen, and the Fatimid caliph al-Mu'izz (d. 975). However, neither of these candidates were viable: the Zaydi Imam had died nine years before Mu'izz al-Dawla conquered Baghdad and it is extremely unlikely that the Buyids would have wanted a Fatimid caliph in Baghdad if they were concerned about maintaining their own power. Worse, Ibn al-Jawzi did not correctly identify the Fatimid caliph reigning in 945, who was al-Mansur. Instead, Ibn al-Jawzi named the Fatimid caliph al-Mu'izz, who did not come to power until 953, eight years after Mu'izz al-Dawla conquered Baghdad. In short, Ibn al-Jawzi's account of tenth-century sectarianism is unreliable. We cannot trust it to provide even basic facts of chronology, much less an informative analysis of Sunni–Shi'i relations under the tenth-century Buyids. Neither of the tenth-century Sunni sources discussed the decision by

Mu'izz al-Dawla to depose the 'Abbasid caliph. The story was mentioned in Miskawayh's Buyid-sponsored history, but he attributed the decision to political motivations without religious overtones. The Sunni sources dating to the period after the fall of the Buyids were more concerned with the Shi'i identity of the Buyid amirs than the contemporary sources.

Contemporary Sunni sources reacting to the Shi'i Buyid control over Baghdad and the Sunni 'Abbasid caliph do not appear to be predominately concerned about the Shi'i identity of the Buyids. These contemporary sources emphasize other local problems, such as popular religious movements and the overall decline in religious knowledge among experts. Not until the thirteenth and fourteenth centuries do accounts of Buyid history begin to emphasize the sectarian nature of their reign.

How Can the History of Islamic Sectarianism Help Us Understand Contemporary Events?

As this book has argued, the historical development of Muslim sectarian identities was a long and complex process. While Sunnis and Shi'is have not always gotten along, they have peacefully coexisted more often than not. Even during the tenth century, when most of the Muslim world was ruled by Shi'i dynasties, there were not broad anti-Shi'i attitudes apparent among non-Shi'i Muslims. Thus, when modern discussions of sectarianism in the Middle East reduce these identities to a fourteen-hundred-year war between Sunnis and Shi'is, we create a false narrative of near-endless conflict that leads us to conclude that these fights are timeless, unchanging, and impossible to combat. The current sectarian conflict in the Muslim world is largely a legacy of colonialism, especially the period when the British and French emphasized divisions amongst the peoples of the Middle East in order to perpetuate internal conflicts which would make the region easier for them to control. Today, this false narrative of sectarian hostility has been fuelled by recent events such as competition between Sunni Saudi Arabia and Shi'i Iran.

The Saudis follow a conservative interpretation of Sunni doctrine known as Wahhabism. A Saudi religious leader, Muhammad ibn 'Abd al-Wahhab (d. 1792) articulated this doctrine in the eighteenth century: he preached against common Muslim religious practices, such as the veneration of saints, the visiting of their tombs, and requests for intersession on the Day of Judgement. More significantly for our purposes, the Wahhabi movement was also virulently anti-Shi'i: Wahhabi forces sacked a significant Shi'i shrine (Karbala) in 1802 during a Shi'i holiday, killing approximately two to five thousand Shi'is and plundering and damaging the shrine there, dedicated to Husayn b. 'Ali, the son of 'Ali. While many contemporary Muslims consider Wahhabi ideology extreme, the Wahhabis became an influential force in the region due to their political alliance with the Saud family (now the royal family of Saudi Arabia). Ibn Saud created the Kingdom of Saudi Arabia in 1932 and the Saudis struck oil in 1938, providing them with a crucial source of wealth to fund Wahhabi teachings around the world.

While the Wahhabi movement has always vilified Shi'is, the 1979 revolution in Iran, which led to the creation of a Shi'i state led by Ayatollah Ruhollah Khomeini (d. 1989), exacerbated these tensions. Before the revolution, Iran was ruled by a secular leader, Mohammad Reza Shah Pahlavi (d. 1980), who was known for the violence of his secret police and oppressive policies directed at the Iranian peoples. The revolution which overthrew the Shah was made up of a broad coalition of opposition forces. After the revolution, however, Ayatollah Khomeini and his followers came to dominate the new government of Iran, arguing that Iran should be ruled via the guidance of Shi'i religious scholars. After the revolution, Ayatollah Khomeini declared that the revolution had awakened Shi'is worldwide. Iran funded various Shi'i Islamist movements in other countries, such as in Lebanon, Iraq, Afghanistan, Pakistan, Bahrain, and Saudi Arabia.

Saudi funding of extremist Wahhabi movements worldwide and Iranian financial support of Shi'i movements within other Muslim countries has exacerbated sectarian tensions in the region and sectarianised political and economic competition. These contemporary conflicts are not a result of an endless hatred between Sunnis and Shi'is but caused by complex social, economic, and political forces.

As a historian, I would argue against ever trying to draw a straight line between events in the ninth and tenth centuries to explain events in the Middle East today. The period under consideration in this book saw the birth of the Muslim community and its development into a complex society. Understanding the development of different Muslim identities and the history of Islamic sectarianism can temper our facile conclusions about the supposed timelessness of sectarian conflict.

Notes

[52] Adam Mez, *The Renaissance of Islam*, trans. Salahuddin Khuda Bukhsh and D. S. Margoliouth (London: Luzac, 1937), 59.

[53] C. E. Bosworth, "The Early Ghaznavids," in *The Cambridge History of Iran*, vol. 4: *The Period from the Arab Invasion to the Saljuqs*, ed. R. N. Frye (Cambridge: Cambridge University Press, 1975), 176.

[54] Al-Muqaddasi, *Ahsan al-Taqasim fi Ma'arifat Al-Aqalim* in *Bibliotheca Geographorum Arabicorum*, vol. 3, ed. M. J. de Goeje (Leiden: Brill, 1906), 1–2. Al-Muqaddasi's *Ahsan al-Taqasim* was translated by Basil Anthony Collins as *The Best Divisions for Knowledge of the Regions* (Reading: Garnet, 2001). In this chapter, when providing in-text citations of al-Muqaddasi, I will cite Collins' translations.

[55] For Nizam al-Mulk, I will be citing the *Siyasat-nama* as translated by Hubert Darke (London: Routledge & Kegan Paul, 1960).

[56] Al-Maliki, *Riyad al-Nufus*, ed. Bashir al-Bakkush, 3 vols. (Beirut: Dar al-Gharb al-Islami, 1981–84) 2:49.

[57] Ibn al-Jawzi, *Muntazam*, 6:394 and 7:10 as well as Ibn al-Athir, *al-Kamil*, 8:179.

[58] Ibn al-Jawzi, *Muntazam*, 7:15–16 and 14:151. Ibn al-Athir, 8:407; Ibn Kathir, *al-Bidaya wa al-Nihaya*, ed. Editing Board of al-Turath, 15 vols. (Beirut, Dar-Ihya' al-Turuth al-Arabi, 1993), 9:259 and 11:243), 9:259 and 11:243.

[59] Ibn al-Athir, 8:148–49.

Glossary of Key Terms

Abu Bakr (d. 634): First successor to the Prophet Muhammad, who led the Muslim community in Medina from 632–634 CE. Shi'is view him as having usurped power from 'Ali b. Abi Talib.

'Abbasids: Dynasty that came to power in 749–750 in a revolution that overthrew the previous 'Umayyad dynasty. The 'Abbasids arose out of a revolutionary underground movement that fed on proto-Shi'i sentiment and the frustration of non-Arab Muslims. Once in power, they founded the city of Baghdad as their new capital and began to distance themselves from the proto-Shi'i demands of their revolution. They are known for the overall Persianization of the Muslim empire. While they were under the military authority of the Buyids and the Seljuks during several periods, their rule lasted until the Mongols conquered Baghdad in 1258.

Achaemenids: Iranian empire from ca. 550–330 BCE, founded by Cyrus the Great. Created a centralized Persian state that strongly influenced the development of Persian identity in Iran.

'Adud al-Dawla (d. 983): Regnal name of Fanna Khusraw, the Buyid amir from 949–983. He was the son of Rukn al-Dawla and successor of his uncle 'Imad al-Dawla. He was the amir of Fars in southwestern Iran and then took over Baghdad. He adopted ancient Iranian modes of authority (such as taking the title "Shahanshah") while trying to Arabize and Islamicize the heritage of the Buyids.

Aghlabids: Dynasty in North Africa (800–909) who nominally ruled for the 'Abbasid caliphs before being overthrown by the Fatimids.

Ahl al-Sunna: Literally translates to "the people of tradition" and often used as a term to denote early religious scholars who devoted themselves to collecting *hadith.*

Ahura Mazda: Translates to "Wise Lord," the name of the Creator God of Zoroastrianism. See also: Zoroastrianism.

'**Ali b. Abi Talib** (d. 661): Cousin and son-in-law of the Prophet Muhammad, as well as his fourth successor as caliph (r. 656–661). Shi'i Muslims consider him the rightful successor of the Prophet and regard him as the first Imam.

'**Arib b. Sa'd** (d. ca. 980): Maliki author in Cordoba who wrote an account of Fatimid rule based on reports of Maliki refugees from North Africa. Selections of his work can be found in Ibn 'Idhari's chronicle.

'Alid: Term used to describe descendants of the Prophet Muhammad via his cousin and son-in-law 'Ali b. Abi Talib and Fatima, the daughter of the Prophet. *'Alids* have a special status in Shi'i belief. All of the Shi'i Imams are *'Alids*.

Bahram Gur (d. 438): The Sassanid Shah Bahram V. Best remembered for being reared at the Arab Lakhmid court of al-Hira and then winning the crown of the Sassanids with an Arab army.

Banu Dhabba: According to legend, one member of this Arab tribe settled in the Daylamite region of Iran.

Batin: Translates to "hidden" or "inner." The term is often used in Shi'ism and Sufism to mean the hidden meaning of the Qur'an.

Batini: Term sometimes used by Sunnis to describe Shi'is due to a perceived stress on the *'batini'* meaning of the Qur'an by Shi'is.

Bayaniyya: No longer extant proto-Shi'i movement formed by early eighth-century followers of Bayan ibn Sam'an, an Arab from Kufa. They supported the Imamate of Abu Hashim, the son of Muhammad ibn al-Hanafiyya, and engaged in esoteric speculation about the Qur'an.

Berbers: Indigenous ethnic group of North Africa which today prefers the term *Amazigh*, meaning "free people." Many Berbers were early converts to Islam but felt they were treated as second-class Muslims; they revolted against 'Umayyad rule in 739–40 and established some semi-independent kingdoms in North Africa. In their rise to power, the Fatimids recruited heavily from the non-urban Berbers of North Africa.

Buyids: Dynasty of Persian Shi'i Muslims from the Daylamite region of Iran, just south of the Caspian Sea. Founded by 'Ali b. Buya after his conquest of Fars in 934. Ruled Baghdad, the capital of the 'Abbasid caliphate, from 945–1055. Under 'Adud al-Dawla, the Buyids claimed descent from the Persian Sassanid shahs. They are best remembered as Persian Shi'i rulers who 'captured' the Sunni 'Abbasid caliph and his capital.

Byzantine Empire: The continuation of the Roman Empire. Historians tend to use the term "Byzantine" to describe the Christianized Roman Empire after the capital moved from Rome to Constantinople in the fourth century. Until the Byzantines were conquered by the Ottomans in 1453, they tended to control Anatolia and act as both competitors and allies of Muslim empires in the Middle East.

Caliph: Translates roughly to successor or caretaker. The title of caliph was taken by the successors of the Prophet Muhammad to denote the religious and political leader of the Muslim community.

Companions of the Prophet: Designation for the community of Muslims who knew the Prophet Muhammad during his lifetime. In Islamic history and legal jurisprudence, the testimony of trusted Companions on issues related to the Prophet and the interpretation of the Qur'an can be considered authoritative.

Darius the Great (d. 486 BCE): Achaemenid king of Persia who built the famous terrace and palaces of Persepolis, the Achaemenid capital.

Daylam: Mountainous region of Iran, just south of the Caspian Sea. Residents of the region are known as "Daylamites" and were often rumoured to be uncivilized, brutal warriors. The Buyids originated from the Daylam.

Farr: Zoroastrian concept of divine favour or royal glory that symbolically linked Iranian rulers with the splendour and fortune of Ahura Mazda, the Zoroastrian god. A powerful source of legitimacy which 'Adud al-Dawla attempted to tap into in articulating his own authority.

Fatima: (d. 632) Daughter of the Prophet Muhammad; wife of 'Ali b. Abi Talib; mother of Hasan and Husayn, the third and fourth Shi'i Imams; the namesake of the Fatimid dynasty.

Fatimids: Isma'ili Shi'i dynasty (909–1171) which rose to power in North Africa, declared a rival caliphate, and eventually expanded to control most of North Africa, Syria, Palestine, and the holy cities of Mecca and Medina. Founded the city of Cairo as their capital.

Ghayba: Often translated as "occultation," the belief that one of the descendants of the Prophet (usually someone considered an Imam in Shi'ism) has disappeared and remains in a state of spiritual hiding but will return to usher in the end of times. Twelver Shi'is specifically believe that the twelfth Imam, Muhammad al-Mahdi, remains in a state of *ghayba.*

Ghaznavids: Turkic dynasty from Central Asia which ruled large portions of Iran, Afghanistan, and Transoxiana from 977–1186. Mahmud of Ghazni was their best-known ruler.

Hadith: Accounts of the words and actions of the Prophet Muhammad. These are used as an important source of Islamic law.

Hamdanids: Dynasty in northern Iraq and Syria who competed with the Buyids for control in the tenth century.

Hanafism: One of the four Sunni schools of jurisprudence, named for the scholar Abu Hanifa (d. 767). It was prevalent in North Africa when the Fatimids rose to power.

Hanbalism: One of the four Sunni schools of jurisprudence, named for the scholar Ahmad ibn Hanbal (d. 855). Ibn Hanbal has been remembered in medieval Islamic history for refusing to conform to the Caliph al-Ma'mun's religious decrees during a period known as the *Mihna.*

Hashimiyya: Proto-Shi'is who followed the Imamate of 'Abd Allah ibn al-Hanafiyya, also known as Abu Hashim, who was the eldest son of Muhammad ibn al-Hanafiyya. The Hashimiyya eventually supported the 'Abbasid family and played a significant role in supporting the 'Abbasid Revolution.

Hijra: Event in 622 when the Prophet Muhammad and the fledgling Muslim community emigrated from Mecca to Medina to form the first Muslim settlement.

Hilal ibn al-Muhassin al-Sabi (d. 1056): a bureaucrat and historian who served the Buyid amirs. He wrote a history of the rules and protocols of the 'Abbasid court, *Traditions of the Caliphal Court* (*Rusum Dar al-Khalifa*), which are a significant source of late tenth and early eleventh century attitudes about the Buyids.

Husayn (d. 680): the grandson of the Prophet Muhammad and the son of 'Ali b. Abi Talib. Best remembered for his martyrdom at the Battle of Karbala (680). Now considered the third Imam in most Shi'i traditions.

Ibn Abd al-Wahhab, Muhammad: see Wahhabi.

Ibn al-Athir (d. 1233): Sunni historian who composed *al-Kamil fi'l-ta'rikh*, a universal history that emphasized the sectarian nature of Buyid rule in Baghdad.

Ibn al-Jawzi (d. 1200): Sunni Hanbali legal scholar who helped craft later views of Sunni orthodoxy and Shi'i heterodoxy. Lived and wrote in Baghdad in the twelfth century. He is most famous for his *al-Muntazam fi ta'rikh al-muluk wa al-umam*, a multi-volume universal history, which emphasized the sectarianism of the Buyid amirs.

Ibn Kathir (d. 1373): Sunni religious scholar and historian in Syria. His fourteen-volume universal history, *al-Bidaya wa al-Nihaya*, portrayed the tenth century as a period of great sectarian tension and violence.

Ibn al-Muqaffa' (d. 756): Courtier who served the 'Abbasids and composed the earliest surviving Muslim work on ideal kingship, emphasizing that the ideal king maintained stability and established religious orthodoxy.

Ibn Idhari (d. after 1313): Moroccan scholar who wrote *al-Bayan al-Mughrib*, a history which portrayed the Fatimids in terms of sectarian conflict.

Ibn Saud (d. 1953): Founder of the modern state of Saudi Arabia and its first king. Known for his sponsorship of Wahhabi doctrine.

Imam: In a Shi'i context, the Imams represent descendants of the Prophet Muhammad chosen by God to lead the Muslim community in the absence of a prophet. Nearly all Shi'i groups agree that the first Imam was 'Ali b. Abi Talib.

Imamiyya: a broad term used for early Shi'is who sought to follow the guidance of an Imam. Sometimes used today as a term to describe the Twelver Shi'is in particular, although they are not the only Shi'i sect who follow an Imamate.

Isma'ili: A form of Shi'ism which split from the other Imamiyya in the eighth century over the designation of the successor to Ja'far al-Sadiq (d. 765). The Isma'ilis followed his son, Isma'il (d. ca. 762), while the group that later became known as the Twelver Shiʻis followed his half-brother, Musa al-Kazim (d. 799).

Jaʻfar al-Hajib (d. fl. tenth century): the chamberlain of the first Fatimid caliph, al-Mahdi (d. 934), who made the trip from Syria to North Africa with al-Mahdi. Wrote an account of his journey, the *Sirat Jaʻfar al-Hajib.*

Janahiyya: No longer extant proto-Shiʻi movement which followed Ibn Muʻawiya. They ascribed to the controversial belief that God was incarnate within their leaders, beginning with Adam. When Ibn Muʻawiya died, the movement split into several groups.

Kaisaniyya: No longer extant proto-Shiʻi movement which followed the Imamate of Ibn al-Hanafiyya. They were probably the first group to believe in the idea of the return of the *Mahdi.*

Kharijism: Literally translated as "those who leave," the *Kharijis* abandoned the caliph ʻAli b. Abi Talib at the Battle of Siffin (657). The name *"Khariji,"* however, is controversial. Instead, they use the term *shurat* (exchanger) or *Muhakkima* for themselves. The Ibadis are surviving members of this community.

Khomeini, Ayatollah Ruhollah (d. 1989): The first Supreme Leader of the Islamic Republic of Iran. Emphasized the need to export the Shiʻi Islamic Revolution, which had ended the rule of the Shah in Iran in 1979, and funded Shiʻi movements in other countries. Khomeini's support for revolutionary Shiʻi movements in other states increased Sunni–Shiʻi hostility in the modern Middle East.

Khurramism: Iranian religious movement that blended aspects of Islam with pre-existing practices and beliefs of Zoroastrianism. Some scholars consider it to be a popular form of Zoroastrianism, while Patricia Crone has argued recently that it is a Zoroastrian-Muslim hybrid where Persian Muslims nativised Islamic beliefs and practices and combined them with existing popular beliefs.

Al-Khushani (d. 981): Sunni Maliki religious scholar who lived in Qayrawan when the Fatimids conquered the city in 909. Left Qayrawan in 923 to resettle in Spain and serve the court of the Sunni ʼUmayyads. His biographical dictionary of Sunni religious scholars, *Akhbar al-fuqaha wa al-muhaddithun*, provides an important source of Sunni reactions to Fatimid rule.

Khutba: a type of speech or sermon given at the mosque during the community Friday prayer. *Khutba*s often provide important information for how medieval leaders viewed themselves and their community.

Lakhmids: Arab kingdom in southern Iraq from ca. 300–602 CE. Their capital was al-Hira and they were often allies or clients of the Sassanid Empire. The Lakhmid king, al-Mundhir I, helped raise the Sassanid Shah, Bahram Gur, and retake his throne after his father was assassinated.

Madrasa: Muslim religious schools or colleges, which helped spread concepts of religious orthodoxy. The origin of the *madrasa* has usually been traced to patronage by the caliph and other political elites in the eleventh century, after the fall of the Buyids, as a way of training Sunni Muslim bureaucrats to work for the state. However, there were informal modes of education before the rise of the official *madrasa*.

Mahdi: Literally translated as "guided one," the *Mahdi* is an eschatological redeemer who will return to earth and bring justice before the Day of Judgement. Many early proto-Shi'i religious leaders claimed to be the *Mahdi* or a spokesperson for the *Mahdi*.

al-Mahdi, 'Abd Allah (d. 934): The first Fatimid caliph and the Isma'ili leader who shifted the movement from an underground organization to an open revolutionary movement that established a Shi'i caliphate.

al-Mahdi, Muhammad: The figure whom the Twelver Shi'is believe is the final Imam. He disappeared soon after his birth and Twelvers believe that he will return to usher in the Day of Judgement.

Mahmud of Ghazna (d. 1030): Best known ruler of the Ghaznavid dynasty in eastern Iran, Afghanistan, and modern Pakistan. A Sunni ruler who used his faith to rationalize invading Buyid territory in order to save the 'Abbasid caliph from the Shi'i Buyids.

al-Maliki, Abu Bakr (d. 1148): A Sunni Maliki scholar who lived in Qayrawan after the era of Fatimid rule. His work, *Riyad al-Nufus*, portrayed the Fatimids as exacerbating sectarian tensions within the city.

Malikism: One of the four Sunni schools of jurisprudence, named for the scholar Malik ibn Anas (d. 795), which was prevalent in North Africa when the Fatimids rose to power.

Al-Mansur billah (d. 953): The third Fatimid caliph. Defeated a local *Khariji* rebellion and founded a new capital city in North Africa: *Mansuriyya*. He followed 'Abbasid precedents in his claims to legitimacy, including the choice of his regnal name.

Al-Mansur (d. 775): The second 'Abbasid caliph, who is usually regarded as the true founder of the 'Abbasid dynasty. He built the 'Abbasid capital of Baghdad.

Mansuriyya: No longer extant proto-Shi'i movement centered in Kufa which followed Abu Mansur al-'Ijli (d. ca. 740). Abu Mansur claimed to receive prophecy. The group is often best remembered for their violent tactics. (Not related to the Fatimid city called *Mansuriyya*.)

Mazdakism: A sixth-century Zoroastrian reform movement which followed the leader ship of Mazdak the Younger (d. ca. 524). Later Khurramism was linked with Mazdakism.

Mihna: A period from 833–848 when the 'Abbasid Caliph al-Ma'mun tried to enforce a particular view of Qur'anic interpretation.

Mughiriyya: A no longer extant proto-Shi'i movement which was strongly influenced by gnostic and Manichean doctrines. Also known for their esoteric interpretations of the Qur'an.

al-Mu'izz (d. 975): The fourth Fatimid caliph who conquered Egypt and founded the new Fatimid imperial capital of Cairo to commemorate their success.

al-Muqaddasi (d. ca. 1000): a scholar from Jerusalem who travelled the Middle East between the years of 965–985, during the zenith of Fatimid and Buyid rule. He wrote *The Best Divisions for Knowledge of the Regions* (*Ahsan al-Taqasim fi Ma'rifat al-Aqalim*) to provide a resource for "devout and upright people" who might draw upon the story of his travels for entertainment or profit. In general, he portrayed Fatimid and Buyid rule in a positive light.

Al-Muqtadir (d. 932): Controversial Abbasid caliph who came to power when he was only thirteen years old. The second Fatimid caliph al-Qa'im attacked him as the "youth not yet mature…who… governs Islam" and used him as evidence that the 'Abbasid caliphs were failing to lead the Muslim community properly.

al-Mutanabbi (d. 965): One of the most famous Arab poets. The Buyid amir 'Adud al-Dawla was one of his patrons and he wrote praise poetry helping to explain the Persian ruler to an Arab audience.

Miskawayh (d. 1030): An official who served the Buyids and, under the direction of ʿAdud al-Dawla, wrote *The Experience of Nations* (*Tajarab al-Umam*), which chronicled Buyid rule in Baghdad.

Nass: Within some groups of Shiʿism, *nass* refers to the designation of the Imam by the previous Imam.

Nizam al-Mulk: Persian scholar and vizier of the Seljuq Empire (d. 1092). Known for his treatise *Siyasatnama* ("The Book of Government"); it explained the role of government in Islamic society.

Persepolis: Capital of the Achaemenid Persian dynasty, founded around 515 BCE. Archaeologists believe that Cyrus the Great selected the site but that it was substantively built by Darius the Great. The capital acted as a ceremonial complex and was especially important for celebrating Nowruz, the Persian New Year. Persepolis held great significance as the symbolic centre of Persian kingship.

Proto-Shiʿi: Term to identify early supporters of the caliphate of ʿAli before a broader identity of "Shiʿi" existed.

Proto-Sunni: Term to identify the supporters of the caliphate of Abu Bakr, before a broader identity of "Sunni" existed.

Qadi: Judge.

Qadi al-Nuʿman (d. 974): The first chief Qadi for the Fatimid dynasty. He was born in Qayrawan and served the first four Fatimid caliphs. He wrote many books on Ismaʿili jurisprudence and scriptural interpretation. His history of the foundation of the Fatimid state, *Kitab iftitah al-daʿwa wa-ibtida' al-dawla* (*The Beginning of the Mission and Establishment of the State*), provides significant information on the establishment of the dynasty.

Al-Qaʾim bi Amr Allah (d. 946): The second Fatimid caliph. He was born in Syria and made the long trip to North Africa with his father. He led Fatimid forces in several attempts to conquer Egypt.

al-Qayrawani, Ibn Abi Zayd (d. 996): A Sunni Maliki who led the Sunni Maliki school of jurisprudence in Qayrawan during early Fatimid rule. He taught, delivered religious rulings, and wrote about Sunni Maliki religious law. His *Kitab al-Jami'* discussed life and religious doctrines for Malikis under Fatimid rule.

Rashidun: Term used by Sunnis for the first four caliphs after the death of the Prophet Muhammad. Means "rightly guided."

Rustamid: *Khariji* Ibadi dynasty established in Algeria in the 770s; it survived there until the early tenth century, when the Fatimids conquered their territory.

Saba'iyya: A no longer extant proto-Shi'i movement from the seventh century which followed Ibn Saba'. Often known as the first *ghulat* and possibly the first to predict that 'Ali b. Abi Talib had not died but was in a state of occultation and would return to his followers.

al-Sabi, Abu Ishaq: Author of a history of the Buyids sponsored by 'Adud al-Dawla which attempted to rewrite the history of the Daylamites to portray them as descendants of both Arabs and Persians.

Sassanids (224–637): Persian empire before the rise of Islam. Succeeded the Parthian empire and was a major competitor with the Roman-Byzantine Empire. The Buyids used symbolism from the Sassanid era to buttress their political legitimacy.

Sayf al-Dawla (d. 967): Hamdanid ruler of Aleppo and another one of the poet al-Mutanabbi's patrons. Also a rival of the Buyids.

Seljuks: A Sunni Turkic dynasty which conquered Baghdad and ousted the Buyids in 1055. In 1071, their defeat of the Byzantines at the Battle of Manzikert began a chain of events that resulted in the Crusades.

Shafi'ism: One of the four Sunni schools of jurisprudence, named for the scholar al-Shafi'i (d. 820).

Shi'at 'Ali: Literally "Partisans of 'Ali." This phrase is the term from which we derive the word "Shi'i."

Shi'i: One of the major sects of Islam. While there are several significant branches with different beliefs and practices, Shi'is overall believe in a line of Imams who were sent to guide the world in the absence of a living prophet.

Shi'i Century: Term often used to describe a period in the tenth century when two Shi'i dynasties (the Fatimids and the Buyids) rose to power.

Sufism: Islamic mysticism.

Sunna: Traditions of the Prophet Muhammad and his Companions. See also *Ahl al-Sunna*. The term "Sunni" derives from the phrase *Ahl al-Sunna wa al-Jama'a*, which translates as "the people of tradition and consensus."

Sunni: One of the major sects of Islam. While there are several significant branches with different beliefs and practices, Sunnis overall believe in the legitimacy of the caliphs who ruled after the Prophet Muhammad.

Sunni Revival: Term often used to describe the period after the Shi'i Century, when Sunni dynasties retook political control over the Middle East.

Al-Tabari (d. 923): Scholar and historian who wrote *Tarikh al-Rusul wa al-Muluk* (*History of the Prophets and Kings*), which is one of the best known medieval histories of Islam.

Al-Tanukhi (d. 994): Sunni religious scholar who served the Buyid amirs in various positions. Author of a history of tenth-century Baghdad society, *Nishwar al-muhadarah wa akhbar al-mudhakarah.* While Al-Tanukhi was a Sunni religious scholar, he did not comment on the Shi'i identity of the Buyids, instead focusing on a broad deterioration of religious knowledge among Sunni religious scholars and the growing popularity of Sufi movements.

Twelver Shi'is: The most numerically prevalent form of Shi'ism today. Often also known as the *Imamiyya*. See also Muhammad al-Mahdi.

'Umar b. al-Khattab (d. 644): The third caliph after the death of the Prophet Muhammad. Regarded by Sunnis as one of the Rightly-guided caliphs. He was also often known as the "the Just Ruler" (*al-Sultan al-'Adil*) and portrayed as the quintessential Arab in historical chronicles. 'Adud al-Dawla chose a title that harkened back to 'Umar's reign, despite the fact that 'Umar was not fondly remembered by Shi'is due to his rivalry with 'Ali b. Abi Talib.

'Umayyads: A powerful clan and the first dynasty after the death of the Prophet Muhammad. While the first 'Umayyad ruler, 'Uthman (r. 644–656), was known for his piety, his powerful family challenged the caliphate of 'Ali b. Abi Talib and took over the rule of the Muslim world from 661–750, when they were overthrown by the 'Abbasids. A second 'Umayyad dynasty was also established in Spain from 756–1031.

Wahhabi: Muslim religious movement founded by Muhammad ibn 'Abd al-Wahhab (d. 1792), which is the dominant ideology in modern Saudi Arabia. Wahhabi doctrine emphasizes the need to return to a pure version of Islam modelled on the practices of the Prophet

Muhammad and eschewing practices which they view as having developed over time, such as the veneration of saints, Sufism, and Shi'ism. The modern Saudi state funds Wahhabi schools and movements throughout the world, which contributes to the modern development of sectarian hostility.

Zaydi: The smallest of the three major modern forms of Shi'ism and the first to split off from the *Imamiyya* and form their own distinct group. Followed the Imamate of Zayd, one of the sons of 'Ali Zayn al-'Abidin, which is why we call them Zaydis. The rest of the *Imamiyya* followed one of Zayd's half-brothers.

Ziyadat Allah (d. 909): Last Aghlabid ruler of North Africa. Portrayed in Fatimid histories as a debaucher and unfit to rule.

Zoroastrianism: One of the world's oldest extant religions, possibly originating in the second millennium BCE. Named for a Persian-speaking prophet named Zoroaster, Zoroastrians follow a deity known as Ahura Mazda (the Wise Lord) and also believe in an evil figure called Angra Mainyu. Zoroastrianism was the state religion of the Sassanid empire. The Buyids used symbols from Zoroastrianism in their attempts to craft an argument for their legitimacy.

Further Reading

Here are some suggestions to continue your reading on the topics discussed in the book.

Al-Azmeh, Aziz. *Muslim Kingship: Power and the Sacred in Muslim, Christian, and Pagan Polities*. London: I. B. Tauris, 1997.

> A broad, comparative analysis of the concept of "Muslim kingship," or the ways that Muslim rulers enunciated and represented their royal power. Al-Azmeh places the Muslim model of kingship within a broader historical and cultural framework. A dense work, but very useful for understanding how early Muslim kingship adopted and adapted pre-existing modes of articulating authority.

Berkey, Jonathan P. *The Formation of Islam: Religion and Society in the Near East, 600–1800*. Cambridge: Cambridge University Press, 2002.

> An excellent overview of the emergence of Islamic tradition which highlights how its creation was a process over time, emerging in and influenced by the panoply of religions of the Near Eastern milieu.

Bierman, Irene. *Writing Signs: the Fatimid Public Text*. Berkeley: University of California Press, 1998.

> Analyses how the Fatimids used "public texts" to address multiple audiences and simultaneously bolster their legitimacy as both Muslim caliphs and Isma'ili Imams. Early Fatimid public writing was limited; official writing was usually limited to writing inside sectarian spaces, such as Shi'i mosques. The later Fatimids, however, used exterior writing on mosques to actively define urban spaces as Shi'i and Isma'ili. An excellent source to learn more about how the Fatimids used public writing on coins, textiles, and buildings to address both the Sunnis and Shi'is whom they ruled.

Bulliet, Richard. *Islam: The View from the Edge.* New York: Columbia University Press, 1994.

A seminal work which argues for how the "edge" of the Islamic world, which Bulliet defines as the places where new Muslims were joining the faith, helped influence and ultimately shape Islam. Bullet criticizes the notion of a Shi'i Century and a Sunni Revival, arguing that these concepts only make sense when Islamic history is viewed from the "centre" or the caliphate and produce a false sense of homogeneity within medieval Islam.

Choksy, Jamsheed. *Conflict and Cooperation: Zoroastrian Subalterns and Muslim Elites in Medieval Iranian Society.* New York: Columbia University Press, 1997.

Explores the interaction between Zoroastrians and Muslims from the seventh century until the thirteenth century. Choksy focuses on both the diversity within Zoroastrianism as well as the varied Zoroastrian reaction to Muslim rule.

Crone, Patricia. *The Nativist Prophets of Early Islamic Iran: Rural Revolt and Local Zoroastrianism.* Cambridge: Cambridge University Press, 2014.

A detailed examination of the Iranian response to the influx of Muslims into Iran. While Crone explores rebellions against Muslim rule, this book is most useful for its analysis of new religious ideas that often blended local religious concepts with Islam.

Daftary, Farhad. *The Isma'ilis: Their History and Doctrines.* 2nd ed. Cambridge: Cambridge University Press, 1990.

The most comprehensive existing account of the Isma'ilis, their history, and religious beliefs.

Donohue, John J. *The Buwayhid Dynasty in Iraq 334 H./945 to 403 H./1012: Shaping Institutions for the Future.* Leiden: Brill, 2003.

A political history of the Buyid dynasty, focusing on the institutions which they created that affected later Muslim states.

Ephrat, Daphna. *A Learned Society in a Period of Transition: The Sunni 'Ulama' of Eleventh Century Baghdad.* New York: State University of New York Press, 2000.

Examines the social organizations and frameworks, such as schools and Sufi orders, which developed in order to teach the Islamic religious and legal sciences. Contains an excellent discussion of how to define Sunni Islam, as well as an analysis of the significance of the *madrasa.*

Haider, Najam. *The Origins of the Shi'a: Identity, Ritual, and Sacred Space in Eighth-Century Kufa.* Cambridge: Cambridge University Press, 2011.

> Superb analysis of the emergence of the idea of Shi'i identity in eighth-century Kufa.

Haji, Hamid, ed. and trans. *Founding the Fatimid State: The Rise of an Early Islamic Empire.* London: I. B. Tauris, 2006.

> A translation of Qadi al-Nu'man's *Iftitah al-Da'wa* (*The Opening of the Mission*) which contains first-hand accounts of how the Fatimids conquered North Africa and established their dynasty.

Hanne, Eric J. *Putting the Caliph in His Place: Power, Authority, and the Late Abbasid Caliphate.* Madison, N.J.: Fairleigh Dickinson University Press, 2007.

> A discussion of the relationship between the 'Abbasid caliph and the military dynasties which came to control the caliphate, such as the Buyids and Seljuks. Hanne argues that, in these situations, the 'Abbasid caliphs were not just powerless puppets.

Hashemi, Nader and Danny Postel, eds. *Sectarianization: Mapping the New Politics of the Middle East.* Oxford: Oxford University Press, 2017.

> This edited volume provides an excellent overview of the modern problem of sectarianism and sectarianization.

Jiwa, Shainool, ed. and trans. *Towards a Shi'i Mediterranean Empire: Fatimid Egypt and the Founding of Cairo.* London: I. B. Tauris, 2009.

> A translation of the sections of al-Maqrizi's *Itti'az al-hunafa'* which covers the reign of al-Mu'izz, the fourth Fatimid caliph.

Klemm, Verena. *Memoirs of a Mission the Ismaili scholar, Statesman and Poet Al-Mu'ayyad Fi al-Din Al-Shirazi.* London: I. B. Tauris, 2003.

> An exploration of the diplomatic interactions between the Byzantines, Buyids, Seljuks, and Fatimids during the reign of the Fatimid caliph al-Mustansir. Klemm focuses on the career of al-Shirazi, an important Isma'ili missionary who operated predominately in non-Isma'ili territories.

Marsham, Andrew. *Rituals of Islamic Monarchy: Accession and Succession in the First Muslim Empire.* Edinburgh: Edinburgh University Press, 2009.

> Analyses the rituals used to formally acknowledge the first Muslim rulers.

Mulder, Stephennie. *The Shrines of the 'Alids in Medieval Syria: Sunnis, Shi'is, and the Architecture of Coexistence.* Edinburgh: Edinburgh University Press, 2014.

> Reveals that shrines devoted to 'Alids in medieval Syria were often unique spaces of exchange and shared piety between Sunnis and Shi'is. This book argues that we need to move beyond a simplistic analysis of sectarian ideological division and examine the complex ways that medieval Sunnis and Shi'is interacted.

Sanders, Paula. *Ritual, Politics, and the City in Fatimid Cairo.* Albany: State University of New York Press, 1994.

> Reconstructs Fatimid political culture from its court rituals, arguing that the Fatimids used ritual to articulate their own legitimacy, challenge 'Abbasid hegemony, and create a ritual *lingua franca* that allowed them to appeal to the diverse population of Cairo. She uses this argument to explore the complex relationship between religious and political authority, focusing particularly on how the city of Cairo itself played a central role in articulating Fatimid religio-political authority.

Tucker, William F. *Mahdis and Millenarians: Shiite Extremists in Early Muslim Iraq.* Cambridge: Cambridge University Press, 2008.

> In-depth analysis of the early Shi'i *ghulat* movements which outlines the doctrines of these groups as well as their historical development.

Walker, Paul, ed. and trans. *Orations of the Fatimid Caliphs: Festival Sermons of the Ismaili Imams.* London: I. B. Tauris, 2009.

> Collection of translated speeches given by the Fatimid caliphs.